The Gospel Advent Book

CHRIS CHAVEZ

WITH

SARAH DAMOFF

ILLUSTRATED BY JEN WINDLE

LUCIDBOOKS

The Gospel Advent Book
Copyright © 2018 by Chris Chavez
Coauthored by Sarah Damoff
Illustrations by Jen Windle
Cover title artwork by Melanie Thornton

Published by Lucid Books in Houston, TX
www.LucidBooksPublishing.com

ISBN-10: 1-63296-267-5
ISBN-13: 978-1-63296-267-6
eISBN-10: 1-63296-276-4
eISBN-13: 978-1-63296-276-8

Special Sales: Most Lucid Books titles are available in special quantity discounts. Custom imprinting or excerpting can also be done to fit special needs. Contact Lucid Books at info@lucidbookspublishing.com.

Heather Chavez, I cannot say the words enough: without you, this family does not work. You are the fun, the love, and the engine that keeps us running. You have put in countless hours producing for our business, allowing me to chase God's purpose in these books. I know it is just for a season, but it has been the long, long season. I look forward to the many chapters of our marriage we have yet to write...together!

—Chris Chavez

To the Anglican Church, who taught me the beauty of the church calendar; to my friend Anne Lincoln, who lovingly ushered me into curriculum writing; to my husband, Luke, whose generosity and theological education are manifest throughout this book; to my children—Naomi, Eliot, and Haven—who teach me the good questions to ask; and to those whose wait is long, whose night is dark, and who desperately thirst for this bright hope of Advent.

—Sarah Damoff

Contents

The Gospel Advent Book

CHRIS CHAVEZ

Introduction

Read to children sometime before beginning the daily lessons.

Every year at this time of the year, many families like ours celebrate Christmas. Christmas isn't mentioned in the Bible, but like many holidays we celebrate, Christmas is a part of our culture. It is the day we celebrate the birth of Jesus. But it is important for you to know that celebrating Christmas is just part of our culture and not a part of the Bible. "Culture" refers to the behaviors and beliefs shared by a group of people. We always need to understand what is biblical and what is not, what is important and what is not, what is true and what is not, and especially where to look for truth. We find truth in the Bible.

Now, the Christmas holiday is only a few hundred years old and not everything we learn from it is true. For instance, Jesus was not even born in December. More than likely, he was born in the spring.[1] But have you ever had a birthday party on a day that wasn't actually your birthday? Or have you ever gone to a friend's birthday party, but the party wasn't actually on his birthday? Did it make the party any less fun because it was on a different day? No…because the day you celebrate is not the point. The point is to celebrate your birth or the birth of your friend. That is the same with Christmas. Just because December 25th isn't Jesus's

---

1. Matt Slick, "On What Day and Month Was Jesus Born?" Christian Apologetics & Research Ministry, accessed August 2, 2018, https://carm.org/on-what-day-month-was-jesus-born.

actual birthday doesn't make it any less exciting. Have you ever seen a picture of three wise men at the manger? Did you know that they didn't bring their gifts until Jesus was about two years old?[2] Crazy, isn't it? As much as we love to celebrate Christmas, we also want you to know what is true and what is not.

So, what we are going to do this Christmas season is celebrate Advent. The word *advent* is Latin and means "coming." Can you say "Advent"? Do you remember what it means? Yes, it means "coming." The word *advent* isn't in the Bible, but we are going to join other Christians around the world to focus on Jesus's coming and celebrate Advent. For many people the celebration of Advent begins four Sundays before Christmas and ends on Christmas Eve. It is a season to remember Christ's first coming, and to anticipate and prepare for Christ's second coming.

This book will teach us about why Jesus's coming is such good news. Does anyone know of another word we use instead of saying "good news"? Yes, "Gospel." *Gospel* means "good news." So, we are going to sing, do activities, memorize Scripture, and really learn more about the story behind Christmas. *The Gospel Advent Book* is going to remind us that Jesus first came as a Jewish messiah. Does anyone know what *messiah* means? A messiah is a promised deliverer or a savior of a people. Jesus is the promised deliverer or messiah of the Jewish people. We don't think about it much, but when Jesus came as a baby, he came to be the King of the Jews. OK, let's see what you think of truth. Does anyone know Jesus's real name? Give me your best guess. Jesus's real name is Yeshua. *Yeshua* actually means "salvation" in Hebrew. So when we get to the part of the story where he comes from heaven, we will call him by his real Hebrew name: Yeshua.

---

2. Bible.org, "The Visit of the Wise Men (Matthew 2:1–12)," accessed August 2, 2018, https://bible.org/seriespage/3-visit-wise-men-matthew-21-12.

But the Good News, as we will learn, will teach us that the Jewish Messiah was always intended to bless all people. God has always been the God of all people. But if we are not Jewish, what does that make us? Can you give me a good guess? Gentiles. Now, does being Gentile mean you are not as good as a Jewish person? Of course not! It only means that there are different characters or groups, just like in most stories. Each group plays their part, and we will discover that because the Jews didn't play their part well, we were blessed.

Note to parents: You might want to look through the daily activities and see if you will need supplies.

Activity Prep:
- Gather/create supplies. As a family, discuss which of the following supplemental supplies might be helpful for you during your Advent devotions, and use today to prepare the supplies you choose. You are free to use as many or as few as fits with your family's desires.
- Create an Advent wreath.
- Create a timeline to be filled in each day.
- Find a Bible with a map in it for reference.
- Create flashcards to write information about the different Bible characters we will talk about.
- Gather individual journals and writing/drawing supplies for any family member who might want to keep thoughts and prayers in a journal as we go through the month.

Song Resource: You will find the lyrics below. There are various versions of this classic song, so we also created a video that will help guide your family as they learn the song. You can search YouTube for "The Gospel Advent Book."

"O Come, O Come, Emmanuel"[3]

Stanza 1—

    Line 1 - O come, O come, Emmanuel,

    Line 2 - And ransom captive Israel,

    Line 3 - That mourns in lonely exile here

    Line 4 - Until the Son of God appear.

Refrain:

    Rejoice! Rejoice! Emmanuel

    shall come to thee, O Israel.

Stanza 2

    Line 1 - O come, Thou Rod of Jesse, free

    Line 2 - Thine own from Satan's tyranny;

    Line 3 - From depths of hell Thy people save,

    Line 4 - And give them victory over the grave.

Stanza 3

    Line 1 - O come, Thou Day-spring, come and cheer

    Line 2 - Our spirits by Thine advent here;

    Line 3 – Disperse the gloomy clouds of night

    Line 4 - And death's dark shadow put to flight

---

3 "O Come, O Come, Emmanuel," traditional Latin hymn, translated by John Mason Neale.

How to Use This Book

This book was designed to help lead your family through daily devotionals during the Advent season. The lessons begin on December 1st, instead of on the traditional first Sunday of Advent. There is one lesson for each day, with the exception of two lessons for Christmas Day (a morning and an evening lesson). This book will walk through select Old Testament stories and use them as teaching tools in order to reveal the true excitement the Advent season should bring. Advent is typically presented without setting a solid Hebrew background that informs the Messiah's coming to a primarily Gentile audience. *The Gospel Advent Book* attempts to connect the dots with a little more clarity. To do this, each lesson follows the same pattern, but you are welcome to take or leave any of the following components according to what is most helpful to your family.

Sing: We will be singing "O Come, O Come, Emmanuel," learning additional lines each day. Lyrics are on page 4, and you can discuss what the lyrics mean as you learn them. *Emmanuel* means "God with us," so we will be singing in anticipation of his coming. We also have a video of the song that will help you learn the flow of the song. You can find it by searching YouTube for "The Gospel Advent Book." Bookmark this webpage and use it as often as needed.

Scripture Reading: If your child or children are old enough to read, you can let them take turns reading. Verses are taken from the English Standard Version, and sometimes it is helpful to refer back to the verses during or after the story.

Conversational Bible Story: The stories are written so you and your child or children can interact during the story. The comprehension questions are incorporated into each story. This will help facilitate learning and keep them engaged. Before you begin each story, you can show your child or children the picture and have them guess what the story might be about. You can also invite them to draw their own pictures or take notes about what they hear while they are listening to the story. Basically, do whatever you feel will help them engage.

Prayer: In this section there are scripted prayers to help you pray along the lines of the story. You are welcome to add to these prayers or lead your family in an entirely different prayer format—whatever is most comfortable for you. In addition to the scripted prayer, it might be helpful to ask if anybody has a certain prayer request or would also like to say a prayer.

Scripture Memory: Over the course of the season, we will memorize a total of three brief verses or passages of Scripture. We will use motions to help with memorization. When you begin a new verse, explain what any unknown words mean as well as whom any pronouns refer to (i.e., "He" = God, etc.). Once people are comfortable saying the verse, have them take turns saying it on their own.

Activity Options: Each day there are between one and three suggested activities. Choose none, one, two, or all of them to do together in order to have fun and reinforce the lesson. Most of them can be done with no supplies or with supplies you already have around your house. The hope is that the activities would never be a burden for parents but rather a simple and enjoyable extension of the lesson.

Creation of the World

Today's Scripture Reading: If your child or children are old enough to read, they can take turns reading the Scripture of the day.

"The heavens declare the glory of God, and the sky above proclaims his handiwork" (Psalm 19:1).

We are going to learn "O Come, O Come, Emmanuel," we will start each lesson by learning and then singing before we read the story.

Sing "O Come, O Come, Emmanuel"

Go to YouTube and search for *The Gospel Advent Book* to watch our video. After watching the video together, you should be able to practice today's assignment.

Learn Stanza 1, Lines 1 and 2.

STORY

Creation of the World (Genesis 1–2)

Do you know what was in the beginning before there was anything else? **God**. There is one true God, and he has always been. In the beginning he created the heavens and the earth. God said, "Let there be light!" Just like that, light shone out of the darkness. God created everything out of nothing, just by speaking it. God created the land, seas, sun, moon, stars, birds of the sky, fish of the sea, land animals, and humans. In six days, God created everything. Who created everything? **God**. How did he create everything? **By speaking**. (Take a minute to try to create something only by speaking.)

The last thing God created was on the sixth day: people. God said, "Let us make man in our image." (Gen. 1:26). He created the first man, Adam, out of the dirt of the earth. Then, out of Adam's rib, God made the first woman, Eve. God made humans to rule over all living things. God told Adam and Eve to be fruitful and multiply. He wanted them to have children and families. What did God create last? **People**. How did God create people? **He made Adam out of the dirt and Eve out of Adam's rib**. What did God tell Adam and Eve to do? **To be fruitful and multiply, which means to have children and families**.

God gave Adam and Eve a perfect garden home, and he gave them everything they needed. Adam and Eve lived freely with God in the garden. God told Adam not to eat fruit from a certain tree called the Tree of the Knowledge of Good and Evil. God warned Adam that if he ate fruit from that tree, death would surely come.

God looked over everything he had made and said, "Very good." What did God say about everything he had made? **That it was very good**. The next day was the seventh day. God rested on that day and called it holy. Do you know what "holy" means? **It means "set apart."** And it is important for us to understand that when we say that God rested, it doesn't mean he was tired. It just means he stopped working. God was finished with the work he set out to do. Do you have any questions about this story?

Alright! You guys did great. Well, each night we will work on memorizing something from the Bible. By the end of our time with this book, we will have memorized three verses. So, let's start off with a nice, easy one.

Memory Verse: If your child or children are old enough to read, they can take turns reading the memory verse of the day.

> *"And he is before all things, and in him all things hold together" (Colossians 1:17).*

Repeat the verse a couple of times all together, and then add motions:
   "before" - use thumb to point behind you
   "all" - stretch arms out wide
   "him" - point upward
   "all" - stretch arms out wide
   "hold together" - clasp hands together

Great job! Don't worry if you didn't do it perfect today. We have a few days, and before long you will be able to do it with no problem.

But before we do anything else, let's take some time to pray.

Pray

Creator God, we praise you for your power, creativity, and goodness shown in the creation of the world. Thank you for making people in your image. We praise you for your wonderful design of families. Help us take good care of the earth, plants, animals, and people around us. Help us to love all people as you love them and to never consider ourselves above others. Help us to follow your example of doing good and creative work for six days and then resting from work on a wholly peaceful seventh day that is set apart. We pray in the name of the Father, of the Son, and of the Holy Spirit. Amen.

Activity Options

Draw or paint one of the days of creation.

Look at an image of Michelangelo's *Creation of Adam* painting.

Go outside and take a walk, or simply sit together. Look around and talk about all of the very good things God made.

Day 2

The Fall

Today's Scripture Reading: If your child or children are old enough to read, they can take turns reading the Scripture of the day.

> *"And God saw everything that he had made, and behold, it was very good.*
> *And there was evening and there was morning, the sixth day" (Genesis 1:31).*

Sing "O Come, O Come, Emmanuel"

Go to YouTube and search for *The Gospel Advent Book* to watch our video again if needed. If you need to, feel free to sing along with the video.

Practice Stanza 1, Lines 1 and 2.

STORY

The Fall (Genesis 3)

Last night, we learned about creation. We learned that God gave Adam and Eve everything they needed. But do you remember the one thing God warned Adam not to do? **God warned Adam not to eat fruit from the Tree of the Knowledge of Good and Evil.** What did God say would happen if they ate fruit from the one forbidden tree? **Death would surely come.**

One day, as Adam and Eve were in the garden, a snake came to them. The snake was really Satan, who is our enemy and the father of lies. The snake came to Eve and asked her, "Did God really say you can't eat from any tree in the garden?" Eve answered him, but her answer wasn't totally correct. Satan knew what he was doing and how to lead her away from God. He got her to doubt God's goodness. Satan told her that she would not die, which was a lie. He led Eve to think that God was keeping something *good* away from them (a beautiful fruit). But we know that God was really trying to keep something *bad* away from them (the death God knew would come from eating that beautiful fruit).

God never keeps good things away from his children. God always wants what is best for us, but Satan always wants what is worst for us. Eve had to decide whether she would believe what God said or believe what Satan said. Who do you think Eve chose to believe?

Eve looked at the fruit again and noticed how delightful it looked. She was being tempted. Do you know what temptation is? **Temptation is when something looks good for us, but it really is not.** Ignoring God's warning, Eve took the fruit into her hands. Then, she took a bite. She also gave the fruit to Adam. Adam had the same choice, to believe God or to be led astray. But he ate the fruit too. Adam and Eve sinned. Sin is any thought or action that does not honor God. Eating the forbidden fruit was the first sin, and it brought sin into our world. What is sin? **Sin is any thought or action that does not honor God.**

The moment Adam and Eve chose to disobey God, everything changed. They suddenly realized they were naked, and they were ashamed. So, they tried to hide themselves from God. Can you hide from God? **No, of course not.** As God walked through the garden, he called to Adam. "Where are you?" Adam answered, "I heard you coming and I was afraid, so I hid myself." God asked them about the Tree of the Knowledge of Good and Evil, and they finally admitted that they had disobeyed.

God cursed the snake and the ground, and God sent Adam and Eve out of their garden home. Eating the fruit God had told them not to eat was sin, and just as God had warned them, death entered the world. Adam and Eve did not die right away, but their bodies began to grow old and decay. One day, they would die. The world that God created was very good, but now sin and death broke that perfect goodness. What came into the world when Adam and Eve sinned? **Death.** What did God do with the snake, Adam, and Eve? **He cursed the snake and the ground, and he sent Adam and Eve out of the garden.**

But that was not the end the story. God was already doing something amazing that Adam and Eve could not understand. Even as he sent them out of the garden, God kindly gave them clothes as a covering and mysteriously said that one day a man like Adam, born of a woman, would crush the snake, sin, and death. That is what we are studying this season: the Advent—or coming—of that man. What will that man do to the snake, sin, and death? **He will crush them.** Do you have any questions about this story?

You guys are doing great. Does anyone remember the memory verse? Let's try it together.

Memory Verse: If your child or children are old enough to read, they can take turns reading the memory verse of the day.

"And he is before all things, and in him all things hold together"
(Colossians 1:17).

"before" - use thumb to point behind you

"all" - stretch arms out wide

"him" - point upward

"all" - stretch arms out wide

"hold together" - clasp hands together

Great job!

Pray

Protector God, we praise you for giving us warnings and instructions that are for our good. Thank you for the Bible so that we can learn how to live in the way that is best for us. Protect us from the lies and confusion that come from Satan. Give us a strong belief in you so that we might not fall into temptation or choose sin. Forgive us when we do sin, as we forgive others who sin against us. Remind us that we can never hide from you and that we never need to. Thank you for your justice and mercy and for the man who crushes sin and death. We pray in the name of the Father, of the Son, and of the Holy Spirit. Amen.

Activity

Play Two Truths and a Lie: Take turns telling everyone three things, two which are true and one which is a lie. Everyone try to guess which one is the lie. Start by giving an example and reminding the children that it will work best if they think of things that Mommy and Daddy do not already know. Parents can go first to demonstrate what to do. After the game, ask your children where we can always look in order to find out what is true whenever someone tells a lie or says something confusing about God—we look in the Bible to find out what is true. (Ex: Read Genesis 1 if someone says the world wasn't really made by God.)

The Flood

Today's Scripture Reading: If your child or children are old enough to read, they can take turns reading the Scripture of the day.

"With my whole heart I seek you; let me not wander from your commandments!
I have stored up your word in my heart, that I might not sin against you"
(Psalm 119:10–11).

Sing "O Come, O Come, Emmanuel"

Go to YouTube and search for *The Gospel Advent Book* to watch our video again if needed. Really try to get the words down. Feel free to sing along with the video.

Learn Stanza 1, Lines 3 and 4.

Practice singing all of Stanza 1.

Great job! This is going to be so fun. When we know the whole song, it would be fun to send this to (insert names of family members) because we won't see them this Christmas. OK, take a look at this picture. What do you think the story is about today? (Make sure you cover the title of the story)

20

STORY

The Flood (Genesis 6–9)

After Adam and Eve sinned and were sent out of the garden, sin became part of their children and part of everyone who has been born since then. In fact, death came to all creation because of that first sin. God had created everything very good, but in time wickedness and fighting were everywhere. God saw all of the plans inside people's hearts, and they were all evil. This made God so sad that he wished he had not ever made man on the earth. God decided to destroy everyone on earth, including all of the plants and animals. What did God decide to do because of the sin covering the earth? **Destroy everyone on earth, including all of the plants and animals.**

But there was one man who was not like everyone else. His name was Noah. He was a man who did good, made God happy, and walked with God. Who was Noah? **Noah was a man unlike everyone else because he did good, made God happy, and walked with God.** God told Noah to build a big, big boat. Do you know what this boat was called? **An ark.** God was going to make it rain so much that the whole earth would flood and everyone would be destroyed. But Noah and his family could stay safe inside the ark.

God told Noah to gather all the animals in pairs, a male and female, and bring them on the ark along with his family. God promised Noah that he and his family and all the animals would be saved if Noah would obey these instructions. What did God promise Noah? **That if Noah obeyed the instructions to build the ark and gather the animals, Noah and his family would be saved from the flood.**

Day after day, year after year, Noah slowly built the ark. Noah waited and trusted God for 120 years! How long did Noah wait and trust God? **120 years!** Can you imagine how much you would have to believe God to build a boat where there is no water? Do you think you could trust God for 120 years without seeing any rain? Well, that is what faith looks like:

being certain of things we cannot see because we know that God never lies or breaks his promises. We believe what God says because of who he is.

We show faith by exercising our belief with our actions. I can put a chair here and you can say that you trust it to hold you—but the only way to *show* your faith is to actually sit down in the chair. (Take a minute to demonstrate this with a chair.) Noah's faith in God led him to trust and obey everything God said, building the ark and waiting for 120 years before he ever saw a drop of rain.

And then finally—drip, drip, drip. It started to rain. After forty days and forty nights of unbelievable storms, the entire earth was flooded. How long did it storm? **Forty days and forty nights.** All of the people and animals who were once on earth were now gone. All of the trees and tall mountains were under water. Everything! Even though God destroyed everything, he kept his promise and saved Noah's family and the animals on the ark. They were the only ones left.

When the waters went down, God promised he would never again destroy the whole earth with a flood. God placed a rainbow in the sky as a sign and reminder of this promise. When Noah stepped off the ark onto dry land, the first thing he did was build an altar and worship God. After the flood, what promise did God make? **That he would never again destroy the whole earth with a flood.** What sign did God give to help his people remember this promise? **A rainbow in the sky.** Have you ever seen a rainbow? Do you have any questions about this story?

Memory Verse: If your child or children are old enough to read, they can take turns reading the memory verse of the day.

"And he is before all things, and in him all things hold together"
(Colossians 1:17).

"before" — use thumb to point behind you

"all" — stretch arms out wide

"him" — point upward

"all" — stretch arms out wide

"hold together" — clasp hands together

Pray

Holy God, you are so patient, kind, and abounding in steadfast love. Thank you for your faithful and generous mercy to Noah and his family. Give us the firm faith Noah had. We praise you because you always keep your promises. You kept your promise to save Noah's family, you keep your promise to never again destroy the earth with a flood, and you will always keep every promise you ever make. Help us worship and believe you like Noah did. We want to walk with you. We pray in the name of the Father, of the Son, and of the Holy Spirit. Amen.

Activity Options

Do a "trust fall" exercise. Stand behind your child. Have her close her eyes and fall backward, trusting you to catch her.

Act out the story of the flood: Give your children fifteen minutes to prepare a performance acting out the story we just read. Parents can choose to help younger children or to simply be an audience member with older children. Another option is for parents to prepare a performance for children!

Paint a picture of a rainbow and talk about how it must have felt for Noah and his family to finally get off the ark and receive this promise from God.

Promise to Abraham

Today's Scripture Reading: If your child or children are old enough to read, they can take turns reading the Scripture of the day.

> *"Know therefore that the LORD your God is God, the faithful God who keeps covenant and steadfast love with those who love him and keep his commandments, to a thousand generations" (Deuteronomy 7:9).*

Sing "O Come, O Come, Emmanuel"

Go to YouTube and search for *The Gospel Advent Book* to watch our video. Try doing it without singing along with the video. Don't worry about being perfect. By the end, you will be surprised how well your family does.

Practice all of Stanza 1 and learn the Refrain

OK, kids, take a guess what today's story is about! (Show them the picture.)

STORY

Promise to Abraham (Genesis 12–22)

The story behind Christmas starts to become clear when God speaks to a man named Abram. God promised Abram land, that he would have children and grandchildren and great-grandchildren, and that all the families of the earth would be blessed through him. Abram was seventy-five years old when God spoke this promise to him. Abram told God he didn't even have a son and that someday one of his servants would be his heir. An heir is someone who gets the wealth or property of an adult who has died. Do you know anyone who is seventy-five years old? Can you imagine God telling them they would be having a son for the first time at that age?

But God told Abram to look up and try to count the stars. God said he would have as many descendants as there are stars in the sky. And through one of them, all the nations of the earth would be blessed. How many children, grandchildren, and great-grand-children did God promise Abram would have? **More than he could count—as many as the stars!** What did God promise to do through one of those descendants? **Bless all the nations of the earth.** Abram believed what God said and it pleased God. Did Abram believe God would keep his promise? **Yes, and Abram's belief was right and pleased God.**

For many years after God spoke his promise, Abram's wife, Sarai, still did not have a child. In fact, because of her old age it was impossible for her to have a child. But when Abram was ninety-nine years old, God spoke to him again and told Abram that he would soon keep his promise. God then changed Abram's name to Abraham, which means "father of many." God also changed Sarai's name to Sarah, which means "princess." What were Abram and Sarai's new names and what do they mean? **Abraham means "father of many" and Sarah means "princess."**

This promise of a child was even more incredible for Abraham to believe now that he and Sarah were even older. How could Sarah have a child now that she was ninety-nine years old? Once again, though, Abraham believed what God said.

A year later, just as God had promised, Sarah gave birth to a son, and they named him Isaac. What did Abraham and Sarah name the son God had promised them? **Isaac.** Do you know anyone who is one hundred years old? Could you believe that God could give them a child for the first time? It is impossible, but that is just how powerful God is. God's power is one reason we can believe that he always keeps his promises. Do you think that God's timing always looks the same as what we might want? **No, it doesn't.** But God's timing is perfect because he alone always knows what is best and when it is best.

By this time in our story, God had also given Abraham the land he had promised. So God had kept his promise to give Abraham land as well as his promise to give Abraham a son. Do you think God will also keep his promise to bless all the nations of the earth through one of Abraham's descendants? We will find out as we keep reading in the coming days! Do you have any questions about this story?

Memory Verse: If your child or children are old enough to read, they can take turns reading the memory verse.

"And he is before all things, and in him all things hold together"
(Colossians 1:17).

"before" - use thumb to point behind you
"all" - stretch arms out wide
"him" - point upward
"all" - stretch arms out wide
"hold together" - clasp hands together

Pray

Perfect Father, thank you for Abraham and Sarah. Thank you that you always keep your promises, even when it is best for us to wait a long time. Your timing is perfect. You never forget or make mistakes. You know everything and do impossible things. Help us remember that you always know what is best and when it is best. Give us faith like Abraham had. Give us happy patience. Bless and comfort those who want to have children but have not been able to. We pray in the name of the Father, of the Son, and of the Holy Spirit. Amen.

Activity

Bake cookies or another dessert together. While you wait for them to bake, talk about why it's important that they are in the oven for just the right amount of time—not too short and not too long—and how this process reminds us that God knows the perfect time and way to keep every promise he makes. It can help us to be patient in trust when we know something good is certainly coming at just the right time. We can remember how loooong Abraham and Sarah had to wait for the fulfillment of God's promise, but then it was fulfilled in God's perfect timing! When your treat is finally ready, invite a neighbor over and enjoy!

Sacrifice of Isaac

Today's Scripture Reading: If your child or children are old enough to read, they can take turns reading the Scripture of the day.

> *"Trust in the LORD with all your heart, and do not lean on your own understanding. In all your ways acknowledge him, and he will make straight your paths" (Proverbs 3:5–6).*

Sing "O Come, O Come, Emmanuel"

Go to YouTube and search for *The Gospel Advent Book* to watch our video.

Practice Stanza 1 and the Refrain

You are doing great! Does anyone know what the name Emmanuel means? It means "God with us." We are singing for Emmanuel, "God with us," to come because we are learning about the coming of Yeshua (Jesus). He is God the Son. So as we learn this song, we are singing for Yeshua to come and fix the broken world.

STORY

The Sacrifice of Isaac (Genesis 22)

Abraham was one hundred years old when his wife, Sarah, gave birth to their son, Isaac. God had told Abraham that his descendants would be as many as the stars in the sky. Then one day, God tested Abraham. God told Abraham to sacrifice Isaac.

Back then, to sacrifice meant to take an animal, cut it up, and burn it on an altar. People often offered sacrifices to their fake gods. Abraham had offered many animal sacrifices to the one true God, but he would never have considered sacrificing a person. That's unbelievable. But what did God tell Abraham to do? **Sacrifice his son Isaac.**

You would think Abraham might question God about sacrificing his own son. Instead, Abraham trusted that God always knows best and does best. Do you remember what it means to have faith? **It means trusting what God said because of who God is.** Abraham was filled with faith, and he left early the next morning with Isaac and some wood for the sacrifice. They went to Mount Moriah, which was the place where God had told Abraham to sacrifice Isaac. Did Abraham wait to obey God, or did he obey right away? **He obeyed right away.**

Close your eyes and imagine this scene until I tell you to open your eyes. Imagine Abraham and Isaac going up the mountain. As they go up the mountain, Isaac asks his father, "Where is the lamb for the sacrifice?" Abraham answers, "God will provide." When they get to the place God had told Abraham about, Abraham builds an altar, ties up his son, and lays Isaac on top of the wood. Abraham then takes the knife and is about to obediently sacrifice Isaac.

Right at that moment, an angel yells, "STOP! Do not hurt the boy! Now I know you will not keep anything from God." As Abraham looks up, he sees a ram caught in some bushes. So, Abraham takes the ram and sacrifices the ram as a substitute for Isaac. You can open your eyes now. What happened right after Abraham took the knife to kill Isaac? **An angel**

told Abraham to stop and not hurt the boy. What did Abraham then see in the bushes that he sacrificed as a substitute for Isaac? **A ram.**

Just like Abraham said, God did provide a sacrifice for himself. But it was not Isaac. Instead, God provided a substitute. What is a substitute? **A substitute is something that takes the place of another thing.** The ram was a substitute sacrifice.

The angel told Abraham, "Because you did not hold back your son, I will bless you. Your descendants will be more than the stars in heaven." When they had started up the mountain, Abraham did not know what was going to happen. But Abraham trusted God and passed the test. Trusting God can be hard, especially when we do not understand or cannot see how something will end up. But God is always trustworthy, and he always only does what is best, when it is best, how it is best, and where it is best. Do you have any questions about this story?

Memory Verse: If your child or children are old enough to read, they can take turns reading the memory verse of the day.

Who thinks they can do the memory verse on their own?

> *Give everyone the opportunity to try the verse by himself or herself. "And he is before all things, and in him all things hold together" (Colossians 1:17).*

"before" — use thumb to point behind you
"all" — stretch arms out wide
"him" — point upward
"all" — stretch arms out wide
"hold together" - clasp hands together

Now, don't forget this verse, because tomorrow we will start learning a new one. But, you will have the opportunity to recite Colossians 1:17 in a few days.

Pray

Provider God, you are better than anything and anyone else in the world. You are the one true God. You are always only good. Thank you that you always provide what is needed exactly when and where and how it is needed, just like you did for Abraham and Isaac. You always keep your promises. Help us to trust and obey you even when we cannot see or understand what is going to happen. May we treasure you above everything and everyone else that we love. Give us more and more of the gift of faith, so that we can walk by faith and not by sight. We pray in the name of the Father, of the Son, and of the Holy Spirit. Amen.

Activity Options

Serve someone you know who needs provision. Think together about someone who needs an example of the "ram"—something they need but can't get for themselves and are trusting God about while they wait. Oftentimes, God meets the needs of his people through his people. Examples of this could be someone who needs a warm meal, a winter coat, a place to stay, money, a job, a ride to church, help with homework, a friend, etc.

Play a trust game. Go outside and partner up. Have one partner close their eyes or put on a blindfold and the other lead the first person around. It can be scary and confusing not to see or understand where we are going, but it helps when someone we trust is leading us. Many times, we cannot see or understand what is happening in our lives, but God leads us and is always perfectly trustworthy and good.

Day 6

Joseph

Today's Scripture Reading: If your child or children are old enough to read, they can take turns reading the Scripture of the day.

"And we know that for those who love God all things work together for good, for those who are called according to his purpose" (Romans 8:28).

Sing "O Come, O Come, Emmanuel"

If you haven't bookmarked our video on YouTube or our website, make sure you do so. It is a great resource for helping the kids (and you) learn the song.

Practice Stanza 1 and the Refrain

38

STORY

Joseph (Genesis 37–46)

Do you remember the name of Abraham's son? **Isaac.** Isaac grew up and had twin sons named Esau and Jacob. God chose Jacob to fulfill his promise to Abraham. Jacob grew up and had twelve sons. (If helpful, take a minute to draw a family tree.) Jacob loved one of his twelve sons more than the others. That son's name was Joseph.

Jacob made Joseph a marvelous, colorful robe. The robe made Joseph's brothers jealous. In fact, they were more than jealous—they were angry. Why were they jealous and angry? **Because Jacob made a splendid, colorful robe for his favorite son, Joseph.**

Then, Joseph told his brothers about a dream God had given him. In Joseph's dream, God had showed him that one day he would rule over his brothers and even his parents. This made his brothers even angrier than they were before. What did God show Joseph in a dream? **That one day, Joseph would rule over his family.**

Because they got so jealous and angry, Joseph's brothers made a bad choice. They stripped him of his beautiful robe, tore it up, dipped it in blood, and told a lie to their father that an animal had killed Joseph. But really what had happened is that they sold Joseph as a slave and he was taken to Egypt. Do you know what a slave is? **A slave is a person who is forced to obey and do work for someone.** After being forced to be a slave, life got even worse for Joseph. Eventually, someone blamed him for something he hadn't really done, and Joseph wound up in prison.

While Joseph was in prison, God helped him explain what another prisoner's dream meant. Later, Pharaoh had a dream that confused him, too. Does anybody know who Pharaoh was? **He was the king and ruler of Egypt.**

Someone told Pharaoh that the slave and prisoner, Joseph, could explain the dream. God helped Joseph understand Pharaoh's dream—it was a warning from God. Joseph said the dream meant that famine was coming. Do you know what a famine is? **A famine is when there is not enough food in a large area to feed all the people.** How was Joseph able to understand and explain the meaning of this dream? **God gave Joseph the understanding.** As you can imagine, Pharaoh did not want a famine to affect his people. But Joseph also gave instructions about how to store extra food so they would be prepared for the famine and the people wouldn't starve. Pharaoh was happy when Joseph told him how to take care of the land and people. In fact, he was so happy that he made Joseph second in command over all of Egypt. That meant that Pharaoh was the ruler of Egypt, and right there ruling Egypt beside Pharaoh was Joseph.

Joseph stored up extra food so that there would be enough food during the famine. When the famine came, just as God had said it would, people came from everywhere to buy food. Some of the people who came in need of food were Joseph's own brothers—the ones who had jealously sold him into slavery.

When the brothers came to buy food, they didn't recognize Joseph because they were bowing down to him, just like he had dreamed all those years ago. Even though they didn't recognize Joseph, he recognized them. How would you guess he felt and responded?

Joseph showed great love and forgiveness to his family. With tears in his eyes, he told them that he was their brother Joseph. He told them that even though they had hurt him, God had used that painful journey as a way to send Joseph ahead of them so that he could eventually save his family and many other people from dying of starvation.

When Joseph was suffering as a slave and then as an innocent prisoner, did he know what was going to happen? **No, he didn't.** He had to wait a long time for God to act. He had to trust that God was with him, even when life felt very, very difficult and unfair. God was always with Joseph, eventually using what was meant for bad (Joseph's brothers selling him into slavery) to bring good through Joseph in the saving of many people's lives. Do you have any questions about this story?

Memory Verse: If your child or children are old enough to read, they can take turns reading the memory verse of the day.

> *"The LORD is my strength and my song, and he has become my salvation;*
> *this is my God, and I will praise him, my father's God, and I will exalt him"*
> *(Exodus 15:2).*

"Lord" – point upward

"strength" – flex your muscles

"song" – hold an open hand to your mouth as if you were yelling to someone

"salvation" – make a cross with your arms

"my" – point to yourself

"praise" – stretch arms upward in worship

"father's God" – point to your father and/or point upward

"exalt" – wave arms upward in worship

Pray

God of mercy and justice, you are the God of Abraham, Isaac, and Jacob. And you are our God. We thank you that all things work together for the good of those who love you. We confess that it can be hard to trust you and wait for you when we don't know how things will end up. Help us to remember that you do not ever look away from us even for one minute. Give us the patience, faithfulness, trust, understanding, and mercy that Joseph had. Protect us from sinful anger and jealousy, and instead appoint good deeds for us to do so that we might take part in the saving of lives. We ask that through your people you would set slaves free and feed those who are hungry. We pray in the name of the Father, of the Son, and of the Holy Spirit. Amen.

Activity Options

Plant a seed. When you plant it, talk about how it *appears* that you're just getting rid of it, burying it in the darkness of the dirt. But the seed first must go into the dark in order to later sprout and have beautiful life in the light. Talk about the parallels between the seed and Joseph's life. Meditate on how we can hide these truths in our heart so that we have a firm ground of patient trust to stand on when we go through suffering that we don't understand.

Act out the story of Joseph: Give your children fifteen minutes to prepare a performance acting out the story we just read. Parents can choose to help younger children or to simply be an audience member with older children. Parents can also do a performance for their children. Try to find or create the prop of a colorful robe for this performance.

Research and **make a list** of nations that are struggling with famine today. Look into reputable organizations that work toward feeding people who are hungry. **Pray** for them and **talk about** the possibility of **making a donation** to these efforts instead of or in addition to some of your Christmas gifts.

Birth and Adoption of Moses

Today's Scripture Reading: If your child or children are old enough to read, they can take turns reading the Scripture of the day.

"When the child grew older, she brought him to Pharaoh's daughter,
and he became her son. She named him Moses, 'Because,' she said, 'I drew him
out of the water'" (Exodus 2:10).

Sing "O Come, O Come, Emmanuel"
    Practice Stanza 1 and the Refrain
    Learn Stanza 2, Lines 1–2

44

STORY

Birth and Adoption of Moses (Exodus 1–2)

Jacob, along with all his sons and their families, moved to Egypt with Joseph to escape the famine in their homeland. These were God's chosen people, the Hebrew people, and they had children, grandchildren, and great-grandchildren until there were many Hebrew people in Egypt.

After many years passed, none of the Egyptians remembered Joseph or knew that a Hebrew man had saved Egypt from a deadly famine. The Egyptians forced the Hebrew people to become slaves. Eventually, one Pharaoh ordered all of the male Hebrew babies to be thrown into the Nile River and killed. He did this because of how many Hebrew people were now in Egypt. He was afraid that they might become too numerous and powerful enough to stop working as slaves. What happened to the Hebrew people in Egypt? **They were forced to work as slaves.**

One of the Hebrew mothers hid her new baby son for a few months in order to keep him alive. When she couldn't hide him anymore, she put him in a basket and placed him in the Nile River. Her daughter, the baby's big sister, watched from a distance. Pharaoh's daughter found the baby crying in the basket. Do you remember who Pharaoh was? **The king of Egypt.** So, the king's daughter found the baby. She knew he was a Hebrew baby, and she felt sorry for him. The baby's big sister then asked Pharaoh's daughter if she should go find a Hebrew woman to feed and care for the baby. Pharaoh's daughter said yes and ended up paying the baby's own mother to feed and take care of him while he was very young!

Pharaoh's daughter adopted him and named him Moses. Does anyone know what adoption is? **Adoption is when a parent raises another parent's child as their very own son or daughter.** Adoption happens after the child's first parents are not able to take care of the child, so the child is brought into a second family to be loved and cared for as a son or daughter. Moses's mother knew that the Egyptians would kill him if he was with her, and she knew that the only place he would be safe was with a mother who was not Hebrew. What did Moses's mother do to save his life? **She hid him and put him in a basket in the river, where he was found and later adopted by Pharaoh's daughter.** Do you have any questions about this story?

Memory Verse: If your child or children are old enough to read, they can take turns reading the memory verse.

"The LORD is my strength and my song and he has become my salvation; this is my God, and I will praise him, my father's God, and I will exalt him" (Exodus 15:2).

"Lord" – point upward
"strength" – flex your muscles
"song" – hold an open hand to your mouth as if you were yelling to someone
"salvation" – make a cross with your arms
"my" – point to yourself
"praise" – stretch arms upward in worship
"father's God" – point to your father and/or point upward
"exalt" – wave arms upward in worship

Pray

Good Father, we praise you because you are a perfect heavenly Dad. Thank you for putting it in the hearts of Moses's birth mother and adoptive mother to save his life. We pray now for any babies in our world today whose lives might be in danger, that you would save and help them. Show us how we can be a part of this work, Lord. We ask you to give strength and grace to birth parents as well as adoptive parents. Bless the families of the world. Bless the children of the world. Please act through your people to establish kind lawmakers and just laws on the earth. Comfort those parents who have lost children. We pray in the name of the Father, of the Son, and of the Holy Spirit. Amen.

Activity

Look together at pictures from when your children were babies. Talk about how much joy it brought when they became part of the family and how much love you felt. Think together about how brave Moses's mother was to protect him as a baby and to set him in a basket in the water. Even though Moses's mother didn't know what exactly would happen, God always knew about the family Moses would be born into, the family he would be adopted into, and the important work he would do for his people's freedom when he grew up (which we will learn about tomorrow). In the same way, God knows where each of us come from and where we are going.

Day 8

The Burning Bush and the Plagues

Today's Scripture Reading: If your child or children are old enough to read, they can take turns reading the Scripture of the day.

"Then the LORD said, 'I have surely seen the affliction of my people who are in Egypt and have heard their cry because of their taskmasters. I know their sufferings'" (Exodus 3:7).

Sing "O Come, O Come, Emmanuel"
Practice Stanza 1, the Refrain, and Stanza 2, Lines 1–2

STORY

The Burning Bush and the Plagues (Exodus 2–11)

Even though Moses grew up in Pharaoh's household, he still had concern for his people, the Hebrew people. One day, he saw an Egyptian beating up one of the Hebrew slaves. Moses, thinking nobody would see him, killed the Egyptian and hid the dead body. Do you think Moses was following God's plan or his own plan? **He was following his own plan.**

But when Pharaoh found out what Moses did, he wanted to kill Moses as punishment. So, Moses ran away and hid in the land of Midian, where he got married and had children.

Back in Egypt, the Hebrew people kept crying out to God, begging to be rescued from slavery. God heard their cries because God always hears and pays attention to his children.

One day, the angel of the LORD spoke to Moses from a bush that was on fire but miraculously was not burning up. He told Moses that he was sending Moses back to Egypt to deliver his people out of slavery. How would you feel if God spoke to you that way?

Moses was scared, and he said everything he could think of so that God would send someone else. But Moses was God's choice. Moses was thinking about his fear and weakness, but God reminded him that *he* was going to be with Moses, and that *he* would be the one doing the strong and powerful miracles. God was kind to tell Moses that his brother, Aaron, could go with him. Moses asked God what his name is, and God said, "I AM." Where did God say he was sending Moses? **Back to Egypt.** Why? **To deliver his people from slavery.** What mysterious name did God say when Moses asked God's name? **I AM.**

So Moses did what God said and went back to Egypt. Moses had been away from Egypt for a long time. There was a new Pharaoh. Moses and his Hebrew brother, Aaron, went to the new Pharaoh again and again, asking Pharaoh to let God's people go on a three-day journey to make sacrifices and worship the LORD in the wilderness. Pharaoh said, "I do not know the LORD, so I will not obey him! And the people cannot leave for three days! They must keep working! In fact, I am going to make their work even harder now and punish them when they do not do it well!" Moses did not understand how this was helping deliver God's people, and he wished he hadn't been sent to them if it was only to see Pharaoh cause them even more pain. How did Pharaoh respond when Moses and Aaron asked if their people could go away for three days? **Pharaoh would not allow it, but instead made their work harder and punishment even worse.**

God then sent plagues to Egypt. Do you know what a plague is? **A plague can be a disease, infestation of pests, or just something that destroys life.** Moses and Aaron would ask Pharaoh to let the people go, Pharaoh would say "no," and God would send a plague on the Egyptians. Pharaoh would then say that the Hebrews could go to the wilderness, but then—once the plague ended—Pharaoh would change his mind again and would not allow them to rest from their work and go on their journey. Each plague showed a different way that God was the only true God and was more powerful than the Egyptians or the gods that the Egyptians worshipped. Nine times God sent a plague and nine times Pharaoh's heart stayed hard against God and God's people.

Finally, God told Moses that after the tenth plague, Pharaoh would let them go. Tomorrow, we will learn about the tenth plague. Do you think God had a plan to save his people? **Yes.** God always has a plan to save his people. He remembered his promise to Abraham. Do you have any questions about Moses or this part of the story?

Memory Verse: If your child or children are old enough to read, they can take turns reading the memory verse of the day.

> *"The LORD is my strength and my song and he has become my salvation; this is my God, and I will praise him, my father's God, and I will exalt him" (Exodus 15:2).*

"Lord" – point upward

"strength" – flex your muscles

"song" – hold an open hand to your mouth as if you were yelling to someone

"salvation" – make a cross with your arms

"my" – point to yourself

"praise" – stretch arms upward in worship

"father's God" – point to your father and/or point upward

"exalt" – wave arms upward in worship

Pray

Our God, the great I AM, thank you that you always hear, see, pay attention to, and respond to your children. Thank you that you knew your people were suffering in Egypt and you sent Moses to deliver them from slavery. Thank you that you do strong and powerful things even through sinful and fearful people—just like Moses and just like us. We pray that you would hear us, especially in times of suffering. We pray that you would bring justice and peace to all your people on the earth today. We pray in the name of the Father, of the Son, and of the Holy Spirit. Amen.

Activity Options

Draw a picture of Moses and the burning bush.

Research reputable organizations that work toward ending slavery in the world today. **Pray** for them and **talk about** the possibility of **making a donation** to these efforts instead of or in addition to some of your Christmas gifts. One recommended organization is International Justice Mission (IJM), and there are many others!

Day 9

Passover and Leaving Egypt

Today's Scripture Reading: If your child or children are old enough to read, they can take turns reading the Scripture of the day.

"Then Moses said to the people, 'Remember this day in which you came out from Egypt, out of the house of slavery, for by a strong hand the LORD brought you out from this place. No leavened bread shall be eaten'" (Exodus 13:3).

Sing "O Come, O Come, Emmanuel"
Practice Stanza 1, the Refrain, and Stanza 2, Lines 1–2

STORY

Passover and Leaving Egypt (Exodus 12–14)

Last night, we learned that even after God had sent nine plagues, Pharaoh still would not allow the Hebrew slaves a three-day break from their work to go worship God. God told Moses that Pharaoh would let them go after the tenth and final plague, and Moses warned Pharaoh about the tenth plague. Moses told Pharaoh that the LORD was going to pass through Egypt and that every firstborn son would die. What was the tenth and final plague? **That every firstborn son would die.** Over and over Pharaoh refused to listen to God. But on this night, God would show that he always had the power. Everyone would know that there is one true God, the God of Abraham, Isaac, and Jacob.

Before the final plague, God told Moses how the Hebrews could make sure that death passed over their homes so that none of them died. God's people were to take a perfect lamb, kill it, and put some of the blood on the doorposts of their homes that night. The lamb would die instead of the firstborn son. The lamb's death would be a substitute. Do you remember another story we talked about when an animal died as a substitute? **The story of Abraham and Isaac. A ram was the substitute for Isaac.**

The people were then supposed to eat the roasted lamb and dress up as if they were ready to leave. All God's people obeyed and did just as Moses told them to do. The blood of an unblemished lamb covered each doorpost of each home, sealing life in and keeping death out. What did God tell Moses that the Hebrew people should do so that death would pass over their homes? **Put the blood of a lamb on their doorposts.**

That night, on what they called the Lord's Passover, the LORD passed through the land and killed all the firstborn sons in Egypt. But wherever he saw lamb's blood, he passed over and kept that home safe from death. Every firstborn son in Egypt died, even animals. There was not one Egyptian household where someone was not dead. Their cries were heard throughout the land, but the Hebrew children were kept safe. What happened that night to the Egyptian families? **The firstborn son of each Egyptian family died.** What happened that night to the Hebrews? **When God saw the lamb's blood on the doors of the Hebrew homes, he passed over those homes and kept those families safe from death.**

The Pharaoh lost his firstborn son that night. You can imagine how powerless and sad he felt. The next day, Pharaoh told Moses to take the people and leave. After they began the journey out of Egypt, Pharaoh changed his mind again and decided to take his army to chase after and kill God's people.

The direction that God had led them to travel seemed like a mistake at first because God's people were trapped with a big sea, named the Red Sea, in front of them and Pharaoh's army coming behind them. God commanded Moses to lift up his staff and stretch it over the sea. When Moses did that, God divided the waters of the sea into two standing walls of water on each side of a dry pathway, and the people passed through the sea on dry land! When the Egyptians chased them, thinking they could overpower them with their army, God commanded Moses to lift up his staff again, and this time all the waters crashed back down on the Egyptian army.

When the Hebrews were trapped with the sea in front of them and Pharaoh's army behind them, what did God do when Moses lifted up his staff? **He divided the waters of the sea into two walls of water on either side of them, with a path of dry land through the middle for them to walk through.**

Each year on the same day, God's people took time to celebrate the Lord's Passover, just like we celebrate a birthday or any holiday. They needed to remember how God had delivered them from slavery into freedom. They did not yet understand that Passover was a shadow of another perfect sacrifice whose blood would cover and cleanse people from a death they deserve. What was the yearly feast called that God's people celebrated to remember how

God had passed over their homes and had set them free from slavery? **The Lord's Passover.** Do you have any questions about this story?

Memory Verse: If your child or children are old enough to read, they can take turns reading the memory verse of the day.

> *"The LORD is my strength and my song and he has become my salvation; this is my God, and I will praise him, my father's God, and I will exalt him" (Exodus 15:2).*

"Lord" – point upward

"strength" – flex your muscles

"song" – hold an open hand to your mouth as if you were yelling to someone

"salvation" – make a cross with your arms

"my" – point to yourself

"praise" – stretch arms upward in worship

"father's God" – point to your father and/or point upward

"exalt" – wave arms upward in worship

Pray

Oh God of life and death, you are the one true God. We praise you because you are a powerful, mighty, and strong God and you use your power for good. We thank you that you set the slaves free and bring low the people of power who are cruel, wicked, and oppressive. Thank you for the blood of the Lamb that covers your people. Make a way before us when we feel trapped. Soften the hearts of your enemies. Deliver those who are suffering. We pray in the name of the Father, of the Son, and of the Holy Spirit. Amen.

Activity Options

Use clay or Play-doh to make a scene of God's people walking through the Red Sea on dry land. Talk about what that experience must have been like. Try to think together of a time when you felt trapped or hopeless but then God miraculously made a way for you.

Prepare a Passover Seder. If you are not Jewish, do some online research and learn about how this feast is celebrated (check out https://jewsforjesus.org/for-congregations/full-passover-seder-preparation-list/). Prepare some or all of the traditional and highly symbolic foods and settings for this feast, and remember the story of the Lord's Passover together. If you decide to go all out, think about someone you could invite to join you. Another option would be to mark your calendar for the date of the upcoming Passover and look into a place where you could attend a prepared Seder feast.

Ten Commandments

Today's Scripture Reading: If your child or children are old enough to read, they can take turns reading the Scripture of the day.

"You shall therefore love the LORD your God and keep his charge, his statutes, his rules, and his commandments always" (Deuteronomy 11:1).

Sing "O Come, O Come, Emmanuel"
Practice Stanza 1, the Refrain, and Stanza 2, Lines 1–2

62

STORY

Ten Commandments (Exodus 19–20)

After their deliverance from slavery and the miraculous crossing of the Red Sea, the Hebrews walked in the desert for a few months. Then God led the Hebrews to camp at a mountain called Mount Sinai. There God instructed Moses to tell the Hebrews that if they would obey God, then they would be God's treasure among all peoples. They would be a kingdom of priests near to God and a set apart nation. The people answered, "We will do all the LORD asks."

God told Moses to tell the Hebrew people to get ready because in three days God would come down for all the people to see. Three days later, God came down to the mountain just like he had said he would. There was thunder and lightening, thick clouds of smoke, and a very loud trumpet sound. As you can imagine, all of this caused the people to tremble.

Then God said, "I am the LORD God who brought you out of the land of Egypt, out of the house of slavery. You shall have no other gods before me. You shall not carve an idol and worship it. You shall not take the LORD's name in vain. Remember the Sabbath and keep it holy. Honor your father and your mother that your days may be long in the land. You shall not commit murder. You shall not commit adultery. You shall not steal. You shall not bear false witness against your neighbor. You shall not covet your neighbor's house, wife, or anything that is your neighbor's."

These first instructions to the Hebrews were just called the "ten words." We call them the Ten Commandments. After those first ten, God gave them more instructions. In fact, he gave them 613 commands! These rules were to help them live the best and right way. How many commands did God give the Hebrews? **Six hundred and thirteen commands.** Just as the first command that God gave Adam and Eve was a gift to protect their lives, God said that choosing to follow these commands would bring life, while choosing to disobey them would bring death. God wanted them to know how to choose life and be happy.

The Hebrews were no longer just a people. God made them into a nation that day. Do you know what a nation is? **A large group of people living in a certain place and joined together through their history, language, and ways of thinking and living.** They were now the nation called Israel, and God was their king.

God let the people know that the only way to come near God was through a perfect blood sacrifice. A perfect blood sacrifice was needed to cover sin, serve God, or even to praise God. Do you think it would be easy to perfectly obey all 613 commands? **No.** The Israelites were far from perfect, and it did not take them very long at all to disobey many of these commands. That is why a perfect blood sacrifice was needed.

Let's see if we can remember just the Ten Commandments. **(Count with your fingers as the kids name them and see how many they remember.)** Do you have any questions about this story?

Memory Verse: If your child or children are old enough to read, they can take turns reading the memory verse of the day.

"The LORD is my strength and my song, and he has become my salvation;
this is my God, and I will praise him, my father's God, and I will exalt him"
(Exodus 15:2).

"LORD" – point upward
"strength" – flex your muscles
"song" – act like you are conducting a choir
"salvation" – make a cross with your arms
"my" – point to yourself

"praise" – stretch arms upward in worship

"father's God" – point to your father and/or point upward

"exalt" – stretch arms upward in worship

Pray

Holy God above all others, we praise you because you are willing to come near to us. Just like you came near to your people long ago, we ask you to come near to us. Thank you for giving us instructions to live a good life. Help us each day, that we might remember your instructions and follow them. Forgive us when we forget them or make bad choices, and bring us quickly back to your good ways of living. We pray in the name of the Father, of the Son, and of the Holy Spirit. Amen.

Activity

Play an obedience game such as Simon Says, Mother May I, or Red Light, Green Light. Afterward, talk about how hard it is to obey perfectly. Talk about what made it harder or easier to obey during the game (ex: focusing on the one giving the commands versus getting distracted) and how that reflects our relationship with God. Soon we will read the good news that unlocks the shackles of the expectation of perfection.

Day 11

The Tabernacle

Today's Scripture Reading: If your child or children are old enough to read, they can take turns reading the Scripture of the day.

"And let them make me a sanctuary, that I may dwell in their midst" (Exodus 25:8).

Sing "O Come, O Come, Emmanuel"
    Practice Stanza 1, the Refrain, Stanza 2, and repeat the Refrain
    Learn Stanza 2, Lines 3–4

STORY

The Tabernacle (Exodus 25–26)

After God gave Israel the commandments, he also gave Moses instructions to build a tabernacle. A tabernacle is a temporary movable sanctuary, kind of like a big tent. Because it was movable, God would be with the people as they traveled. They were so happy and thankful for being set free from slavery, they joyfully gave their riches and all that was needed to make the place for God to live. The Bible says that when God's people escaped from Egypt, they also got the riches of the Egyptians. It was like God made the Egyptians pay the Hebrews for all the harm they did to them.

God said that this tabernacle would be taken down whenever he moved and put back up whenever he stopped. God would show up as a cloud over the tabernacle by day and as fire by night to lead them. Since their escape from slavery in Egypt, the people had been wandering and traveling, led by God from one place to another and then to another. What was the tent called? **The tabernacle.** What was the tabernacle for? **For God to live with his people as they traveled.**

Each detail of the tabernacle was to be built exactly like God told Moses. Each piece pointed to something greater, just like a shadow points to something greater. (Go into some bright light and point out your shadows to illustrate how the shadow is not real but points to what is real—us.) The tabernacle was filled with shadows of greater things. For example, there was only one entrance to the tabernacle, just like there is only one way into the Kingdom of God.

Near the entrance of the tabernacle was an altar for sacrifice. God always wants to live with his people, and a blood sacrifice is always the first step. The middle of the tabernacle was the most important part. It was called the Most Holy Place. Out of all the people in the world, only one person, from one nation, from one tribe, from one family, and at only one time of the year could enter the Most Holy Place. That person was the High Priest. What was in the middle of the tabernacle, and who could go there? **The Most Holy Place was in the middle of the tabernacle. Only one person could enter there—the High Priest.**

The reason the Most Holy Place was so very special was because of what was inside. Inside the Most Holy Place was something called the Ark of the Covenant. This ark was not a huge boat like the ark we learned about with Noah. Instead this ark was a big wooden chest covered in gold. Do you know what the word "covenant" means? **It means "promise."** Inside this golden chest was where the Ten Commandments were kept. The cover of the ark had two angels facing each other with their wings stretched toward each other. The mercy seat was the area above the wings, and this was the extremely special place where God would be. What was on the mercy seat inside the Most Holy Place? **God.** With this tabernacle, God lived and traveled with his people. Do you have any questions about this story?

Memory Verse: If your child or children are old enough to read, they can take turns reading the memory verse of the day.

> *"In the beginning was the Word, and the Word was with God, and the Word was God" (John 1:1).*

"beginning" — (pretend to) point to your wristwatch
"Word" — make your hands into a book
"with" — make an "OK" sign with both hands and connect them like chain links
"God" — make you hands into a book and lift them to the sky

Pray
God Most High, you are so kind to come near to your people. Thank you for all the shadows that show us more about what you are like. Thank you for making a way to enter your presence, even though you are perfect and we are sinners. Grant that we might continue to see shadows of you in the story of the tabernacle as well as in our daily lives. The confession

of our lips is that we hunger and thirst for the place of your presence. Help us find that narrow way of mercy, and help us also show it to our friends. We pray in the name of the Father, of the Son, and of the Holy Spirit. Amen.

Activity

Create a mini tabernacle by drawing, painting, building, shaping clay, making a blanket fort, etc. Refer to the story or the chapters in Exodus and try to include as much detail as you can. Talk about what it would feel like to have to send your message to God through a High Priest and to have so many requirements to even get close to God to speak with him.

Twelve Spies

Today's Scripture Reading: If your child or children are old enough to read, they can take turns reading the Scripture of the day.

"Now therefore fear the LORD and serve him in sincerity and in faithfulness. Put away the gods that your fathers served beyond the River and in Egypt, and serve the LORD. And if it is evil in your eyes to serve the LORD, choose this day whom you will serve, whether the gods your fathers served in the region beyond the River, or the gods of the Amorites in whose land you dwell. But as for me and my house, we will serve the LORD" (Joshua 24:14–15).

Sing "O Come, O Come, Emmanuel"
Practice Stanza 1, the Refrain, Stanza 2, and repeat the Refrain

74

STORY

Joshua and the Spies (Numbers 13–14)

We have followed God's people on a long journey, and it is not over yet. Remember that a few days ago, we read how God promised Abraham a land. After the nation of Israel agreed to follow and obey God, he led them to that land. The land God promised to Abraham, Isaac, and Jacob was called Canaan. God's people had been foreigners and slaves in Egypt, but Canaan was to be their home. There were other people living in Canaan when they got there—people who were wicked—and God was going to help Israel take the land.

Do you remember how many sons Jacob had? **Twelve.** Those twelve families became the twelve tribes of Israel. So when the Hebrews got to the land of Canaan, God told Moses to select a man from each of the twelve tribes to spy on the land of Canaan. Moses told the spies, "Go and see the land and whether it is good or bad, and whether the people who live there are strong or weak."

When the twelve men came back from spying out the land God had promised, they reported that the land was flowing with milk and honey, which is a way of saying the land is incredibly awesome. But ten of the twelve men gave a bad report, saying the people in the land were too mighty and the cities were too protected for Israel to take the land. Can you believe after all they had seen God do, these men didn't fully trust God?

But there were two men, Joshua and Caleb, who disagreed and gave a good report. Joshua and Caleb said they could and should take the land. They said even if there were giants in the land, they could overpower them with God on their side. What did all twelve spies say about the land? **They said it was a land flowing with milk and honey.** Did all twelve spies agree to enter the land? **No.** Which two spies said they could take the land with God's help? **Caleb and Joshua.** Even after all the miracles God had done for them, the people listened to the ten men and grumbled, saying they should just go back to Egypt. Of course, this made Moses sad. Caleb and Joshua begged the people not to rebel against the Lord, but the people wouldn't listen. Finally, God declared he was going to strike all the people down, but Moses pleaded with God to forgive the people for the sake of his great name. Do you think God is going to forgive them or destroy them?

Well the good news is that God is merciful and abounding in steadfast love. God did forgive the nation, but he also promised that those who decided to disobey his voice would wander the wilderness for forty years and would not enter the land of promise. This would be enough time for everyone of that generation to die. Only Caleb and Joshua would enter the land. What did God say would happen to those who disobeyed his command to enter the land? **God said they would not enter the land and would wander the wilderness for forty years.** I love how merciful God is, but I can't help but notice that there are always consequences for our actions. Do you think God gives consequences to punish people or to teach them so they don't make mistakes in the future? **So they don't make mistakes in the future.** Yes, he gives us directions in his Word and it is always best for us to obey with a good attitude, because following his plans leads to the most joy.

Memory Verse: If your child or children are old enough to read, they can take turns reading the memory verse of the day.

"In the beginning was the Word, and the Word was with God, and the Word was God" (John 1:1).

Give everyone the opportunity to try the verse by themselves.

"beginning" - (pretend to) point to your wristwatch
"Word" – make your hands into a book
"with" – make an "OK" sign with both hands and connect them like chain links
"God" – make your hands into a book and lift them to sky

Pray

God of Abraham, Isaac, and Jacob, you are faithful, keeping every promise. Thank you for leading your people back to the Promised Land after such a long and difficult time. Thank you for responding to Moses's prayer. We praise you for the awesome power you show in forgiveness and love, and confess that often we are like the disobedient Israelites—we only see the scary thing in front of us and forget that a good and powerful God is with us. Deliver us from our fears and increase our belief that we might obey you like Joshua and Caleb. Provide homes to those who need it. Be near to the homeless, the foreigner, and those driven from their homes. We pray in the name of the Father, of the Son, and of the Holy Spirit. Amen.

Activity

Act out the story of Joshua and the spies: Give your children 15 minutes to prepare a performance acting out the story we just read. Parents can choose to help younger children or to simply be an audience member with older children.

Day 13

Entering the Promised Land

Today's Scripture Reading: If your child or children are old enough to read, they can take turns reading the Scripture of the day.

> *"This Book of the Law shall not depart from your mouth, but you shall meditate on it day and night, so that you may be careful to do according to all that is written in it. For then you will make your way prosperous, and then you will have good success. Have I not commanded you? Be strong and courageous. Do not be frightened, and do not be dismayed, for the LORD your God is with you wherever you go" (Joshua 1:8–9).*

Sing "O Come, O Come, Emmanuel"
Practice Stanza 1, the Refrain, Stanza 2, and repeat the Refrain

STORY

Jericho (Joshua 1–6)

Now while Israel was wandering in the wilderness waiting for the disobedient generation to die, Moses disobeyed God as well. Because of his disobedience, Moses did get to see the land of promise, but he wasn't allowed to enter Canaan. So, God chose Joshua, one of the two spies who had given a good report, as Moses's replacement to lead Israel. What did God choose Joshua to do? **Lead the people into the promised land.** God told Joshua that he would be with him, just like he was with Moses, and that no man would be able to stand before him all the days of his life. Doesn't that sound like a great promise before entering a foreign land, that no man would be able to stand before you? Raise your hand if you can tell me the name of the person who led Israel into the promised land of Canaan. **Joshua** (praise and encourage them if they got it.)

Joshua, just like Moses, sent spies to scout out the land, especially the city of Jericho because it was the first city they would have to defeat in battle. The spies were almost captured while in Jericho, but a Gentile woman named Rahab hid them. Do you remember what a Gentile is? **It is anyone who isn't Jewish.** Rahab said the whole city was scared because they had heard of God's great power and might. Rahab knew that God was going to give his people the city, so she asked if they would protect her since she kept them from getting captured. The spies agreed and promised Rahab that if she placed a scarlet cord out of her window, then her whole family would be saved from destruction. The color scarlet is a shade of red similar to the color of blood. So, a cord with a color similar to blood would help save a Gentile from death. Raise your hand if you think God is giving a shadow of something else by using a scarlet cord? **I agree, it is a shadow that blood can save people from destruction.**

God's people were excited to enter the land because the spies reported what Rahab said, that the whole land feared Israel. Now, you might think that God would give Joshua an incredible battle plan. But in order for the Jewish people to know that it was not their strength but God's that would take the city, the plan did not involve a battle at all. Joshua was told to have armed men and priests march around the city once a day for six days. Seven priests would blow trumpets as they carried the Ark of the Covenant. And the people were not to make a sound until the day God would tell them.

So once a day for six days, the armed men and the priests walked around the city. On the seventh day, they marched around the city seven times. On the seventh time, when the priests blew the trumpets, Joshua said to the people, "Shout, for the LORD has given you the city. Only Rahab and her family will live, and everything and everyone else shall be devoted to destruction."

When the people shouted, the mighty walls of Jericho fell down and Israel marched right into the city. They burned the whole city, and the only people to escape were Rahab and her family. Not only did they survive, but they decided to live among God's people the rest of their lives. What I like about this story is that even though it is about Israel, God's special people, God is also showing that he can and will rescue Gentiles who fear his great name.

Memory Verse: If your child or children are old enough to read, they can take turns reading the memory verse of the day.

"He was in the beginning with God" (John 1:2).

"beginning" - (pretend to) point to your wristwatch
"God" - point upward

Pray
Mighty God, we praise you because you are stronger than anything and anyone seen or unseen. We thank you that we can trust you even when things in our life are scary. You brought down the walls of Jericho in power without a battle. Thank you for your mercy to

Rahab and that you made a way for Gentiles and sinners to become part of your people. Grant us trust and help us to obey. We pray in the name of the Father, of the Son, and of the Holy Spirit. Amen.

Activity

Create a mini-city of Jericho using sticks, rocks, blocks, Legos, etc. Reenact what happened at Jericho and talk about times you have seen God be with your family and help you through a "battle."

Samson

Today's Scripture Reading: If your child or children are old enough to read, they can take turns reading the Scripture of the day.

"I love you, O LORD, my strength. The LORD is my rock and my fortress and my deliverer, my God, my rock, in whom I take refuge, my shield, and the horn of my salvation, my stronghold. I call upon the LORD, who is worthy to be praised, and I am saved from my enemies" (Psalm 18:1–3).

Sing "O Come, O Come, Emmanuel"
    Practice Stanza 1, the Refrain, Stanza 2, and repeat the Refrain

STORY

Samson (Judges 15–16)

The Jews, God's special people, conquered much of the land of Canaan under Joshua's command. But when Joshua died, the people began to stray from God's Torah (instructions). Anybody remember how many instructions God gave Israel? **Six hundred and thirteen (the children may say ten commandments, but remind them that those are not all of the instructions or commandments.)** So without strong leadership, Israel followed other gods and fell under the rule of their enemies, just as God said they would.

Do you know what a cycle is? **A cycle is a pattern that repeats over and over.** Well, Israel fell into a cycle: they would follow God for a while, turn from him and follow pretend gods, fall into the hand of their enemy, then cry out to God for help and follow him for a while again. Over and over they did this. Whenever they returned to God, he would raise up a judge. These were men or women God would appoint to deliver and govern Israel. But during this time, everyone did what was right in their own eyes.

One of the judges God gave Israel was a man named Samson. An angel appeared to his mother before he was born and told her she would have a special son. He was to be a Nazarite, which meant he would be totally devoted to God: he could never cut his hair, never touch a dead body, or drink strong drink. As Samson grew, he became incredibly strong. And even though he was one of God's appointed judges, Samson also did what was right in his own eyes.

Samson was strong, so strong that he once killed one thousand of God's enemies, the Philistines, with the jawbone of a donkey. Another time, he tore a lion apart with his bare hands. Samson's problem was not Israel's enemies but following his own way. God wanted to keep his people from being led to follow pretend gods, so he told them to marry only other Israelites. But instead of following God's ways, Samson fell in love with a foreign woman named Delilah. The Philistines used Delilah to trick Samson into telling her the source of his great strength.

The Philistines knew that if they could find out why he was so strong, they could defeat him and rule over God's people. So they promised Delilah a lot of money if she could get Samson to tell her why he was so strong. Over and over she asked Samson, and over and over he lied to her. But Delilah kept nagging him until he told her the truth—that if his hair was cut, he would lose his strength. So as he slept one day—snip, snip, snip—she cut his hair. Samson lost his strength, and with his strength gone he was easily defeated. The Philistines poked out his eyes and put him in chains. What did Delilah do to Samson? **She tricked him into telling the secret of his great strength.**

But as time passed, Samson's hair began to grow back. One day the Philistines took him to their temple to make fun of him. While he was there, Samson prayed to God to avenge the Philistines for the loss of his eyes. Samson grasped the two pillars on which the temple rested, and with the Spirit of God strengthening him again, he pushed the pillars apart and the house fell down on everyone there, including Samson. In his death he killed more of God's enemies than he had in his life.

Memory Verse: If your child or children are old enough to read, they can take turns reading the memory verse of the day.

"He was in the beginning with God" (John 1:2).

"beginning" - (pretend to) point to your wristwatch
"God" - point upward

Pray

Patient God, we praise you because you always pay attention to your people. Thank you for the power you showed through Samson, even after he disobeyed. Help us want to follow your ways because they are good. Any and all strength we have is from and for you. Forgive us when we do not follow your good ways. Guard us from deceit, greed, and pretend gods. Have mercy on us, on our enemies, on those who are leaders, on those who are prisoners, and on those who are blind or disabled. We pray in the name of the Father, of the Son, and of the Holy Spirit. Amen.

Activity

Play arm or thumb wrestling. Talk about Samson and what it means for God to be the source of all our strength. Brainstorm ways that you can use your physical strength to love God.

Day 15

Ruth

Today's Scripture Reading: If your child or children are old enough to read, they can take turns reading the Scripture of the day.

> *"Then they lifted up their voices and wept again. And Orpah kissed her mother-in-law, but Ruth clung to her. And she said, 'See, your sister-in-law has gone back to her people and to her gods; return after your sister-in-law.' But Ruth said, 'Do not urge me to leave you or to return from following you. For where you go I will go, and where you lodge I will lodge. Your people shall be my people, and your God my God'" (Ruth 1:14–16).*

Sing "O Come, O Come, Emmanuel"
Practice Stanza 1, the Refrain, Stanza 2, and repeat the Refrain

92

STORY

Ruth (The Book of Ruth)

Also during the time of God's judges, there was a great famine in the land. Does anyone remember what a famine is? **(Give them time to answer.)** A famine is when there is not enough food in a large area to feed all the people. Because there was a famine, one man from the tribe of Judah moved his wife and two sons from Israel to the land of Moab in search of food. Moab was a land known for great idolatry. Do you know what idolatry is? **Idolatry is what we say when people worship pretend gods or put their trust in anything other than the one true God.** Can you imagine bowing down to a little statue and asking it to take care of you? Well, this practice might sound strange to us, but it is real. In fact, in some parts of the world people still do worship idols today. But idolatry can take many forms—for example, if you have a lot of money, it is easy to put your hope in money instead of trusting in God.

Anyway, as you can imagine, things didn't go well for the man and his family. He soon died, and his two sons eventually married women from Moab instead of marrying Israelite women. After about ten years in Moab, the two sons died as well, leaving the man's wife, Naomi, alone with her two daughters-in-law.

Remember, Naomi was a Jew. Now, when Naomi heard God had visited his people and there was food in Israel, she decided to return home. Naomi advised her daughters-in-law, Orpah and Ruth, to remain in Moab so they could get married again. Orpah listened to Naomi, but no matter how hard Naomi tried to convince Ruth to stay, Ruth promised to go with Naomi. So Ruth, a Gentile, said, "Where you go I will go, and your people shall be my people, and your God my God. Her decision was amazing because she was putting her hope in a God she didn't know. What was the name of the daughter-in-law who decided to return to Israel with Naomi? **Ruth.**

So Naomi and her Gentile daughter Ruth returned to Bethlehem, poor and alone, with no one to watch over them. But Ruth worked hard to ensure they had food. God had given instructions for landowners to allow the poor to gather food during the harvest, so Ruth followed the harvesters in the field every day in order to gather food for herself and Naomi. The story of Ruth's commitment to Naomi spread, and a wealthy man named Boaz took notice. Boaz told Ruth not to go to other fields but to stay in his fields because she would be safe. Boaz also told Ruth that if she needed water, she was welcome to drink freely. When Ruth asked Boaz why he was treating a foreigner so kindly, he said it was because he heard how she had left everything to take care of Naomi. Why did Boaz treat Ruth so well? **Because he had heard how she had left everything to take care of Naomi.**

When Ruth told Naomi about Boaz, Naomi was very pleased because she said that Boaz was a kinsman redeemer for them. A kinsman redeemer was a close relative who could buy back all Naomi had lost and even marry Ruth since her husband had died. Naomi told Ruth exactly the things to do, and it pleased Boaz so much he wanted to redeem them. Boaz followed all the special rules a kinsman redeemer had to follow, and just like Naomi had hoped, Boaz redeemed the land and married Ruth. What makes Boaz and Ruth's marriage different is not just that an Israelite married a Gentile, but that Boaz married a Gentile who chose to follow the one true God. Remember, Ruth had told Naomi, "Your people shall be my people, and your God my God." Ruth truly was a special woman. Soon after, God blessed them with a son they named Obed. Obed was the father of Jesse, and Jesse was the father of David, who became king of Israel. In another story we heard about another Gentile woman named Rahab. Were the two Gentile women Rahab and Ruth better than all the other Gentiles, or did they choose the true God above pretend gods? **They chose God over pretend gods.** Last question. What is the name of the king who came from the family line of Boaz and Ruth? **King David.**

Memory Verse: If your child or children are old enough to read, they can take turns reading the memory verse of the day.

"In the beginning was the Word, and the Word was with God, and the Word was God. He was in the beginning with God" (John 1:1–2).

"beginning" - (pretend to) point to your wristwatch

"Word" – make your hands into a book

"with" – make an "OK" sign with both hands and connect them like chain links

"God" – make your hands into a book and lift them to the sky

"beginning" - (pretend to) point to your wristwatch

"God" - point upward

Pray

Redeemer God, we praise you because you always look after the poor and needy. Thank you for your kindness and justice. Please show us how we can live in a way where the poor and the foreigner can benefit from the fruit of our labor, that we might share all that belongs to us. Please provide for us when we are in need. Thank you for bringing Gentiles into your chosen people. Help us to be like Ruth and forsake all things and to trust in you alone. We pray in the name of the Father, of the Son, and of the Holy Spirit. Amen.

Activity Options

Serve someone in need. At the beginning of this story, Naomi had lost her family and didn't have food. As a family, think of a person you know who might be lonely, hungry, or in need. Pray together about how you could serve that person, and then reach out to them and do so. If you have trouble thinking of someone, ask a pastor if they know someone who needs a meal or some company. Try to choose just one person or family, as opposed to a large mass of anonymous people, and then develop a friendship with the people you choose.

Play a three-legged race. Talk about how it can sometimes be difficult to remain committed to people, like Ruth chose to do with Naomi, but also about why it is worthwhile to do so.

Day 16

King David

Today's Scripture Reading: If your child or children are old enough to read, they can take turns reading the Scripture of the day.

"But the LORD said to Samuel, 'Do not look on his appearance or on the height of his stature, because I have rejected him. For the LORD sees not as man sees: man looks on the outward appearance, but the LORD looks on the heart'" (1 Samuel 16:7).

Sing "O Come, O Come, Emmanuel"
   Practice Stanza 1, the Refrain, Stanza 2, and repeat the Refrain
   Learn Stanza 3, Lines 1–2

98

STORY

King David (Judges, 1 Samuel 8–16)

When we learned about Moses, we found out that God gave his people some land, some instruction, and he was going to be this new nation's king. While following Joshua, Israel conquered much of the Promised Land, but once he died the people fell into a cycle of worshipping pretend gods, falling under the rule of their enemies, returning to God, and then starting the cycle all over.

Eventually Israel lost sight of God's ways. They wanted to be like the nations around them, so they asked for an earthly king. God warned them that a king would be a mistake, but they did not listen. So, God chose a king for them, just as they'd asked. Do you think they wanted a small, ugly king with no teeth and bad breath? Of course not! God chose someone who was very handsome and a head taller than anyone around: Saul. Saul was exactly what most people would want in a king.

For a while, Saul actually was a good king. But it was not long before Saul chose his own way instead of following God's ways. Because Saul's disobedience was so bad, God took the kingdom from Saul and then sought out a man after God's own heart. Which one do you think influences the other—does your heart influence your actions, or do your actions influence your heart? It is the heart that matters. If your heart is right, the actions follow. Saul's problem was that his heart was not right, and God wanted a king with a heart like God's. When King Saul stopped following God's ways, what did God do? **He took the kingdom away from Saul.**

God sent the prophet Samuel to Bethlehem, to a man named Jesse of the tribe of Judah. A prophet is someone God speaks to and then they deliver God's message. God told Samuel that the new king would be from among Jesse's sons. Do you remember Ruth and Boaz? Jesse was their grandson. And in the song "O Come, O Come, Emmanuel," one of the verses talks about Jesse. When Samuel saw Jesse's oldest son, he thought that surely this was whom God had chosen, because he was tall and strong. But God told Samuel that it is not the outside of a person that counts, but the inside. So, Samuel had Jesse bring the next oldest son, but God didn't choose this son either. One by one, Jesse brought seven of his sons before Samuel, but none of them were God's chosen king. So, Samuel asked Jesse if he had seen all of Jesse's sons. Jesse said that the youngest, David, was out watching sheep. God told Samuel that he chose David, and that he must anoint David as king. The Spirit of God rushed upon David from that day forward. Although David was Israel's second king, and he made many mistakes, he was also Israel's greatest king. But God promised there would be another king who would come from David's heritage, and he would be the King of all Kings. What promise did God make? **That there would be another King from David's heritage who would be the King of all Kings.**

Memory Verse: If your child or children are old enough to read, they can take turns reading the memory verse of the day.

> *"All things were made through him, and without him was not any thing made that was made" (John 1:3).*

"all" - stretch your arms out wide
"made" - pretend to be a carpenter using a hammer to make something
"without" - make an "X" with your arms
"not any thing" - shake head "no"

Pray

God who sees, we praise you because you see the heart of every person. You see what is inside each one of us. Thank you for the promise you made about the King of all Kings. We pray for you to help our hearts seek to love your heart, just like David did. Give us the gift you gave Samuel of eyes to see as you do, that we might always remember to pay the most attention to what is on the inside of ourselves and those around us. We pray in the name of the Father, of the Son, and of the Holy Spirit. Amen.

Activity Options

Play the cups and ball game. Set up five colored plastic cups upside down on a table, with a ball under one cup. This should be done when nobody else is in the room. Then invite the family into the room and have everyone take guesses as to which cup the ball is under. Reveal the correct answer and then talk about how they were only able to make guesses because nothing about the appearance of the cups gave away what was inside of them. Next, send everyone out and set the experiment up again, except this time use clear plastic cups. Invite the family back into the room and have them say which cup has the ball inside. People look at the outward appearance, but God always sees what's on the inside of people—their heart and character.

Make two lists to compare possible a) qualities of the outward appearance (e.g., tall, short, big, small, dark, light, etc.) and b) character qualities (e.g., kind, rude, humble, bossy, patient, impatient, selfish, generous, loud, quiet, etc.). Our outward appearance qualities are important, but our character qualities are *most* important.

Solomon Builds the Temple

Today's Scripture Reading: If your child or children are old enough to read, they can take turns reading the Scripture of the day.

"But will God indeed dwell with man on the earth? Behold, heaven and the highest heaven cannot contain you, how much less this house that I have built!"
(2 Chronicles 6:18).

Sing "O Come, O Come, Emmanuel"
Practice Stanza 1, the Refrain, Stanza 2, the Refrain, Stanza 3, Lines 1–2

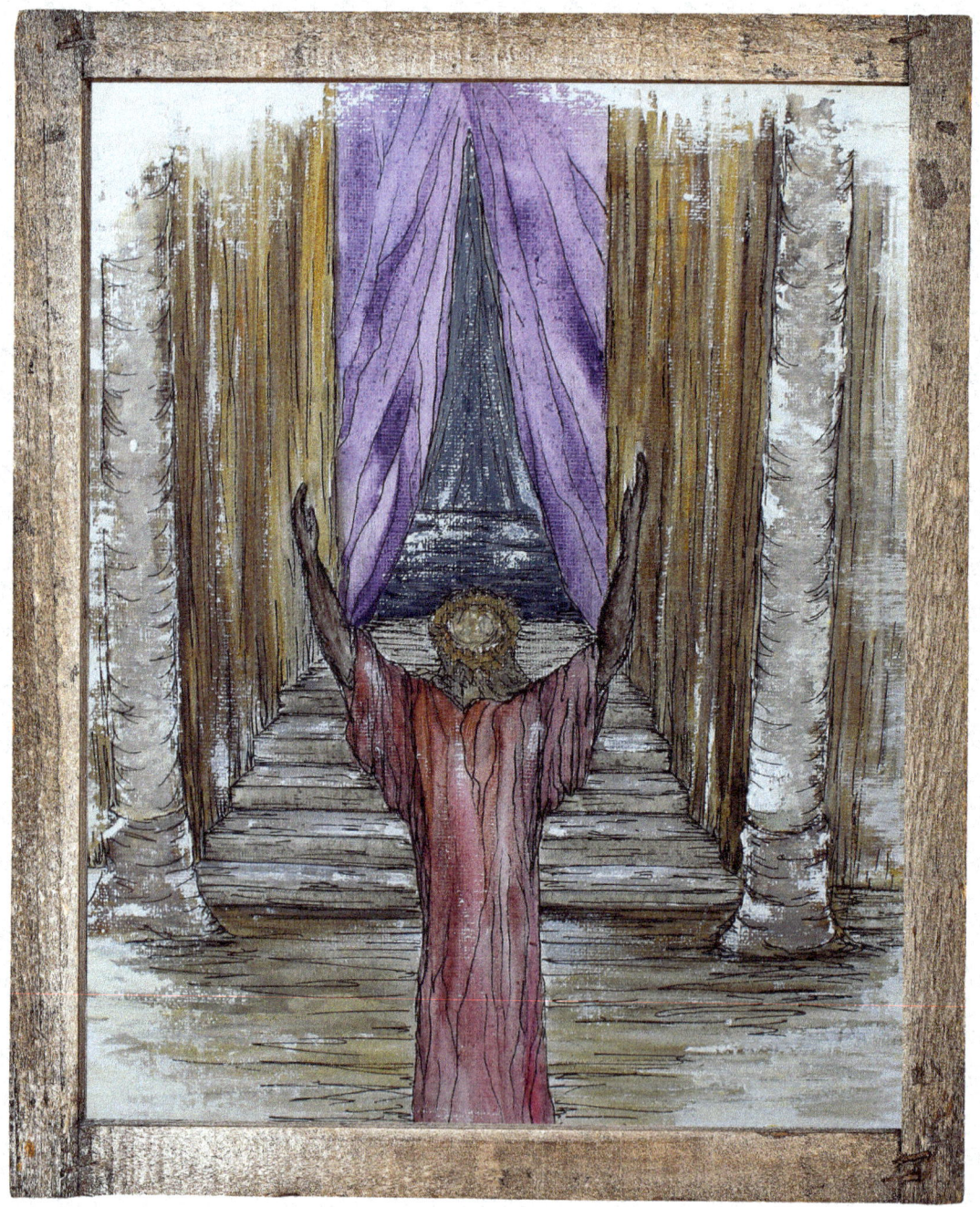

104

STORY

Solomon Builds God's Temple (1 Chronicles 22, 28; 2 Chronicles 1–7, 1 Kings 6)

Four hundred and eighty years after being delivered from slavery in Egypt, the Israelites were finally going to build a permanent temple, where God's presence would dwell. No longer would they have a temporary tabernacle but an actual building in the holy city of Jerusalem. King David loved God and wanted to build God's temple. But since he was a man of war, God told him that his son, Solomon, would be the one to build it. What I love about God is that he cares about our hearts more than we do. When he told David that he wasn't going to build the temple, he also told him that it was good enough that it was in his heart to build it. Isn't God awesome?

OK, so if David wasn't going to build the temple, do you think he did nothing, or do you think he set his son up for success? **(Give them time to answer.)** David, as a man whose heart was like God's, planned ahead and gathered everything Solomon would need, and assigned all the jobs the priests would do. David also told Solomon to gain understanding in order to lead God's people. So when Solomon became king, he followed his father's advice and asked God for wisdom. God not only made Solomon the wisest person who ever lived, but also gave him great riches. Who was Solomon? **David's son, the wisest person who ever lived and the one who built the temple.**

All the plans to build the Temple were patterned after the Tabernacle. Inside the Temple would be the most Holy Place where the Ark of the Covenant would be placed, and God's presence would rest on the mercy seat. This is the place where, once a year on the Day of Atonement, the High Priest would come and sprinkle blood to cover the sins of Israel. This Temple was to be spectacular not just because of all the gold and precious materials, but because God would dwell among his people. What was the Temple? **The place where God's presence would rest.**

The Temple took over seven years to build. When it was finally complete, Solomon dedicated the Temple with prayer by sacrificing thousands of animals, and Israel celebrated for seven days. It was truly an amazing building. God told Solomon that if he would walk in his ways, God would continue to dwell with his people. God also promised that anytime Israel humbled themselves and prayed and turned from their sinful ways, he would forgive their sins. But if they turned from God to idols, he would uproot them from the land he gave them. What did God promise Solomon if the people walked in his ways? **That he would dwell with them and that when they prayed, he would forgive their sins.** What do you think Israel will do—be faithful to God or return to idols? We will have to wait until next time to know for sure.

Memory Verse: If your child or children are old enough to read, they can take turns reading the memory verse of the day.

> *"All things were made through him, and without him was not any thing made that was made" (John 1:3).*

"all" - stretch your arms out wide

"made" - pretend to be a carpenter using a hammer to make something

"without" - make an "x" with your arms

"not any thing" - shake head "no"

Pray

God Most High, we praise you because you alone are wise. Thank you for delighting to give your people wisdom when we ask. We thank you for living among your people. Thank you that you forgive us when we make other things more important than you. You alone are worthy of our worship and praise. We confess that we turn from you far too often and ask you to forgive us and be Lord of our hearts. We pray for you to give us wisdom, that we might know how we should live. We pray in the name of the Father, of the Son, and of the Holy Spirit. Amen.

Activity

Take a drive or look up photographs. Look together at new homes or buildings under construction. If it's possible, do a little research and ask an architect or construction worker about how long it takes to build a new structure from start to finish. Compare that to the seven years it took to build God's Temple. Imagine what it must have looked like and imagine what the celebration must have been like when they were finally done!

Day 18

Division of Israel

Today's Scripture Reading: If your child or children are old enough to read, they can take turns reading the Scripture of the day.

> *"And the LORD was angry with Solomon, because his heart had turned away from the LORD, the God of Israel, who had appeared to him twice and had commanded him concerning this thing, that he should not go after other gods. But he did not keep what the LORD commanded. Therefore the LORD said to Solomon, 'Since this has been your practice and you have not kept my covenant and my statutes that I have commanded you, I will surely tear the kingdom from you and will give it to your servant'" (1 Kings 11:9–11).*

Sing "O Come, O Come, Emmanuel"
Practice Stanza 1, the Refrain, Stanza 2, the Refrain, and Stanza 3, Lines 1–2

STORY

Division of Kingdom (1 Kings 12–15, 2 Chronicles 10–13)

Last night we finished our storytime by wondering if Israel would stay faithful to God or if they would return to worshipping idols. Tonight, we will find out. We left the story with Solomon taking over as king and building the Temple. Sadly, King Solomon's wisdom didn't keep him from marrying foreign women who led him into idolatry. When Solomon led the nation into idolatry, God divided the Kingdom of Israel in two: the Northern Kingdom and the Southern Kingdom. Because of his love for King David, God divided the Kingdom after Solomon's death.

Remember, the nation of Israel was made up of twelve tribes. A tribe is a close group of related families. God had told David that the king would always come from the tribe of Judah, and when the nation split into two, Benjamin was the only tribe that stayed faithful to King David's line of rule. So, the Southern Kingdom was made up of only two tribes: Judah and Benjamin. What two tribes made up the Southern Kingdom? **The tribes of Judah and Benjamin.**

So we know the kingdom was divided, but how did it happen? Well, the division came about through a bad decision by the new king of Israel, Solomon's son Rehoboam. The first thing Rehoboam did was gather the older men for counsel. They told him to remove the heavy tax burden Solomon had on the people. A tax is when the people have to give part of the money they make to the government. We pay taxes and the government makes sure we have roads, policemen, and even schools. But Solomon made the people pay a lot of their money, and the people were tired of it. So, the older wise men told Rehoboam that if he would reduce the tax and be a servant to the people, the people would be loyal to him forever. Do you think he listened? Nope! Instead of listening to them, he gathered young men and asked for their counsel. The young men said the exact opposite, that he should increase the taxes on the people.

When King Rehoboam increased the taxes, ten of the tribes rose up against him and chose their own king. These ten tribes became the Northern Kingdom. The Northern King wanted to make sure the people wouldn't change their minds, so he set up a new capital city and even allowed idols to be set up so the people would not go to Jerusalem. What did the Northern King do to make sure the people did not return to worship in Jerusalem? **Set up a new capital and allow idols.**

Through the years, both the Northern Kingdom and Southern Kingdom had many different kings, some good and some bad. But more and more, both kingdoms fell further into idolatry. God would send prophets, who were his special messengers, to warn them of the consequences for following their own way. But over and over they just would not listen. What happened to the Kingdom of Israel in this story? **It was split into two.**

Memory Verse: If your child or children are old enough to read, they can take turns reading the memory verse of the day.

"In the beginning was the Word, and the Word was with God, and the Word was God. He was in the beginning with God. All things were made through him, and without him was not any thing made that was made"
(John 1:1–3).

"beginning" - (pretend to) point to your wristwatch
"Word" - make hands into a book
"with" – make "OK" sign with both hands and connect them like chain links
"God" – make your hands into a book and lift them to the sky
"beginning" - (pretend to) point to your wristwatch
"God" - point upward
"all" - stretch your arms out wide

"made" - pretend to be a carpenter using a hammer to make something

"without" - make an "x" with your arms

"not any thing" - shake head "no"

Pray

Patient God of Israel, we praise you as the one, true God. Thank you that you know where each one of your people will live. You know every one of our days before any of them happen. We pray lifting up your church today, Lord, that all your people might be united as one people. We pray for ourselves and for your church to be kept from temptation and idolatry, that your name would be known and loved. Help us to have soft, right hearts that love to seek you and to share your goodness, truth, and beauty with all of our friends. We pray in the name of the Father, of the Son, and of the Holy Spirit. Amen.

Activity

Write. Either individually, as a group, or a little bit of both, write a list of a few things that you are sometimes tempted to love and worship more than God. To discern these possible personal idols, think about where most of your time, thoughts, and money are spent. Your list could be different than other members of the family. Next, write down three things that those idols cannot do—but God can. Examples might be, "money cannot forgive sin, but God can," or "new stuff cannot respond to my prayers, but God can." An important note is that the actual thing is not necessarily a bad thing (e.g., wood to make a statue, money, toys, etc.)—what's bad is when that neutral thing is given too great a place in your heart. Pray together for forgiveness of any idolatry that is recognized, and ask God to help you worship him alone.

Jonah

Today's Scripture Reading: If your child or children are old enough to read, they can take turns reading the Scripture of the day.

> *"And the LORD said, 'You pity the plant, for which you did not labor, nor did you make it grow, which came into being in a night and perished in a night. And should not I pity Nineveh, that great city, in which there are more than 120,000 persons who do not know their right hand from their left, and also much cattle?'" (Jonah 4:10–11).*

Sing "O Come, O Come, Emmanuel"
Practice Stanza 1, the Refrain, Stanza 2, the Refrain, and Stanza 3, Lines 1–2
Learn Stanza 3, Line 3–4

STORY

Jonah (The Book of Jonah)

Jonah was one of God's prophets or special messengers. But he was sent to a Gentile city instead of to God's people. Do you remember what a Gentile is? **A Gentile is anyone who is not Jewish.** Nineveh was a wicked city. God sent Jonah there to warn them of God's judgment if they didn't turn from their evil ways. Now Jonah knew God would be gracious and forgive them if they repented, but he didn't want this Gentile city to be forgiven. So rather than obey, Jonah boarded a ship going in the opposite direction. Why didn't Jonah want to go where God was sending him? **He didn't want the city of Nineveh to be forgiven.**

Trying to run from God did not turn out well for Jonah. God caused a great storm that threatened to sink the ship. The fearful sailors cried out to their pretend gods and cast lots to see who was responsible for the storm. Casting lots was an ancient way of finding out what a god thought about a situation. The lot determined that Jonah was the problem. The sailors, wanting the storm to end, asked Jonah what they needed to do. Jonah told them to throw him overboard and God would end the storm. They didn't want to, but they tossed Jonah overboard. And when Jonah hit the water, the storm simply stopped. What did God do when Jonah went the opposite direction? **He sent a storm.**

There Jonah was, in the water and without any way to run from God. So, God sent a great fish to swallow Jonah, and he spent three days and three nights in the belly of the great fish. What do you think it was like inside a big fish? Do you think Jonah was comfortable or that he was uncomfortable? **(Give them time to answer.)** Well, God doesn't mention it, so I can't say for sure, but my guess is that it wasn't fun. God does tell us that, remembering that salvation belongs to the LORD, Jonah cried out to God in prayer. God, being gracious, spoke to the fish, and it spit Jonah up on dry land.

God spoke to Jonah again about going to Nineveh and this time Jonah listened. He went to Nineveh and told them that God would judge them because of their wickedness. Just like Jonah thought, all the people believed and turned from their wickedness. And sure enough, God noticed how they humbled themselves and showed the Gentiles his great mercy by not destroying the city. What did God decide when the people of Nineveh turned from their wickedness? **He did not destroy the city.**

Sadly, Jonah pouted and became angry because God was gracious. God asked Jonah why he shouldn't pity so many people made in his image. And with that, the story of Jonah ends.

Memory Verse: If your child or children are old enough to read, they can take turns reading the memory verse of the day.

"In him was life, and the life was the light of men" (John 1:4).

"life" – make a heart shape with your hands
"light" – make the sun by placing your hands above your head in a circle

Pray

Lord of all, we praise you because you created everything seen and unseen. Even the seas, the skies, and the animals obey you. You created and you love all creation. Thank you for your patience with Jonah and your kind mercy toward the Gentiles in Nineveh. Please forgive us when we think or act like Jonah did, wrongly believing that we are better than someone else or that someone else does not deserve your goodness. We pray for your truth and forgiveness to be known and believed by all people all over the whole world. May we share your love and truth with others, and may our hearts always be ready, willing, and eager to do so. We pray in the name of the Father, of the Son, and of the Holy Spirit. Amen.

Activity

Make a Christmas card. Think of a person or family who may be seen by others the way Jonah unfortunately saw the Gentiles—as unworthy. Jonah just wanted to forget about the Gentiles and ignore them. The person you think of could be someone you personally have wanted to forget about and ignore, or it could be someone that society has wanted to forget about and ignore. Get out your art supplies and create a card for them, wishing them a Merry Christmas and reminding them of how valuable and loved they are as someone made in God's own image. Then pray for that person and send your card. If you have trouble thinking of a neighbor, co-worker, or schoolmate that you know personally, consider making a card for someone at a homeless shelter, nursing home, jail, or children's home.

Elijah on Mount Carmel

Today's Scripture Reading: If your child or children are old enough to read, they can take turns reading the Scripture of the day.

"Answer me, O LORD, answer me, that this people may know that you, O LORD, are God, and that you have turned their hearts back.' Then the fire of the LORD fell and consumed the burnt offering and the wood and the stones and the dust, and licked up the water that was in the trench. And when all the people saw it, they fell on their faces and said, 'The LORD, he is God; the LORD, he is God'" (1 Kings 18:37–39).

Sing "O Come, O Come, Emmanuel"
Practice the entire song

STORY

Elijah on Mount Carmel (1 Kings 18:16–40)

We learned that when the Kingdom of Israel was divided, it was split into two: the Southern Kingdom and the Northern Kingdom. The Northern Kingdom had a lot of kings, and very few of them were good. But one of the Northern Kingdom kings was far worse than any other: Ahab. King Ahab led the people to worship pretend gods. But like always, God sent a prophet to try to bring his people back to worshipping the true God. What did God do to help the Northern Kingdom turn from idolatry? **He sent a prophet.**

The prophet Elijah went to King Ahab and told him to assemble all the people of Israel at Mount Carmel, including the four hundred and fifty prophets of the pretend god Baal. When all the people arrived, Elijah said to them, "If the LORD is God, follow him; but if Baal is God, follow him." So, we have a great battle set up: God's prophet Elijah on one side, and all the prophets of the pretend god Baal on the other side. Who was Elijah? **One of God's prophets sent to help the people return to God.**

Elijah gathered the prophets of Baal and told them, "Get two bulls for us and choose one for Baal. Put it on the wood but do not set fire to it." Remember, Baal was the name of their pretend God. Then Elijah told them that he would prepare the other bull and put it on the wood but would not set fire to it. Then he said, "Call on the name of your god, and I will call on the name of the LORD. The god who answers by fire—he is God."

The prophets of Baal prepared their sacrifice and called on the name of Baal from morning till noon. Do you think Baal responded to them? **No.** Why not? **Idols are just statues made by people.**

By noon, Elijah started making fun of them. "Shout louder! Surely, he is a god! Perhaps he is deep in thought, or busy, or maybe even going to the restroom." But even though they shouted louder, the pretend god Baal did not respond.

So, when it was his turn, Elijah prepared the altar of the LORD and dug a ditch all the way around it. Then, he told them to pour buckets of water on the wood until even the ditch was full of water. Would all the water make it easier or harder for the altar wood to catch on fire? **Harder.**

Then Elijah stepped forward and prayed, "O LORD, God of Abraham, Isaac and Israel, let it be known today that you are God in Israel and that you are turning their hearts back to you again."

Then the fire of the LORD burned up the sacrifice, the wood, and even the water in the trench. When all the people saw this, they fell down and cried, "The LORD—He is God! The LORD—He is God!" What happened when Elijah called on the name of the Lord? **Fire came down right away and burned up the entire sacrifice and altar.**

Sadly, even though the people turned back to God, they soon turned from God again. The same cycle again, just like before. Do you think God will let them continue this cycle forever? We will find out tomorrow.

Memory Verse: If your child or children are old enough to read, they can take turns reading the memory verse of the day.

"In him was life, and the life was the light of men" (John 1:4).

"life" – make a heart shape with your hands
"light" – make the sun by placing your hands above your head in a circle

Pray

God of Heaven and Earth, we praise you because you are the one true God. Thank you for showing your truth and power to your people. Even though we might not bow to statues, we confess that there are many idols we turn toward every day, like getting our way or things that money can buy. Forgive us, and keep our hearts happy to worship you alone. We ask for faith and courage like Elijah had, that other people might know your nearness and power through our lives and our worship. Thank you that you hear and respond to our prayers. No other god can do that. We pray in the name of the Father, of the Son, and of the Holy Spirit. Amen.

Activity

Decorate a Christmas ornament. Make a Christmas ornament with a flame of fire on it to always be a reminder of when the LORD sent his fire down to the altar. Every time you see this ornament, remember this story and that the LORD is God—the only God, the God who is real, powerful, present, active, and paying attention!

Day 21

Exile of Israel

Today's Scripture Reading: If your child or children are old enough to read, they can take turns reading the Scripture of the day.

"When he had torn Israel from the house of David, they made Jeroboam the son of Nebat king. And Jeroboam drove Israel from following the LORD and made them commit great sin. The people of Israel walked in all the sins that Jeroboam did. They did not depart from them, until the LORD removed Israel out of his sight, as he had spoken by all his servants the prophets. So Israel was exiled from their own land to Assyria until this day" (2 Kings 17:21–23).

Sing "O Come, O Come, Emmanuel"
  Practice the entire song

128

STORY

Exile of The Northern and Southern Kingdoms (1 Chronicles 5, 2 Kings 17, 2 Chronicles 22, Deuteronomy 28:62–65, 2 Kings 24)

Last night, we ended our story asking if God would continue the cycle of sin to continue. Today we will find out.

The Northern Kingdom had twenty kings over a couple of hundred years, and none of them did what was pleasing in God's eyes. One thing we can always count on is that he always delivers on his promises. But the nation of Israel had a problem. God did promise to protect Israel from their enemies, but he also promised to remove Israel from the land if they turned from him. God lovingly sent many prophets to warn the people and call the people back to him, but they still set up idols everywhere people would gather. The Northern Kingdom did not listen to the prophets God sent and did not keep his commandments. Did the Northern Kingdom listen to God's prophets? **No.** Because they did not listen, God kept his promise and sent foreign kings to conquer them and scatter them.

Unlike the Northern Kingdom, the Southern Kingdom had a mix of bad and good kings. But just like you would expect, they had a problem with idolatry as well. Even though Jerusalem was the capital and had the Temple, the place where God's presence would actually dwell, the kings allowed places for idol worship in Jerusalem. But even with the fall of the North, and the warnings of God's prophets, the South did not return fully to God either.

Just like he did with the Northern Kingdom, God sent a foreign king to conquer the Southern Kingdom and destroy the Temple. Think about it—God told his people how to build every last detail of the Temple. He had them spend years building the Temple, but then he sent a foreign king to destroy it, the place where his presence dwelled every day for hundreds of years. Then just like that, because of idolatry, God's special people were conquered and exiled. Do you know what it means to be exiled? **To be exiled means to be forced to leave your homeland.** What happened to the Temple and to God's people? **The Temple was destroyed and the people were exiled from the land of Israel.**

This was a dark time in the history of God's people. But the good news is that God still sent his prophets to the people. Not only did the prophets say the exile was coming, but they also prophesied a return to the land one day. Others may dwell in the land, but God gave it as a possession to God's chosen people. Yes, their disobedience caused them to be removed from the land. But God's faithfulness to his Word meant he would fulfill his promise to Abraham, and they would return. During the exile, what did the prophets say would happen? **God's people would return to the land.**

Memory Verse: If your child or children are old enough to read, they can take turns reading the memory verse of the day.

> *"In the beginning was the Word, and the Word was with God, and the Word was God. He was in the beginning with God. All things were made through him, and without him was not any thing made that was made. In him was life, and the life was the light of men" (John 1:1–4).*

"beginning" - (pretend to) point to your wristwatch

"Word" - make your hands into a book

"with" – make "OK" sign with both hands and connect them like chain links

"God" – make your hands into a book and lift them to the sky

"beginning" – (pretend to) point to your wristwatch

"God" – point upward

"all" – stretch your arms out wide

"made" – pretend to be a carpenter using a hammer to make something

"without" – make an "x" with your arms

"not any thing" – shake head "no"

"life" – make heart shape with your hands

"light" – make the sun by placing hands above your head in a circle

Pray

Sovereign Father, we praise you because you are in charge of all the places on earth. Thank you for your patience and your desire to live with your people. So often we make other things more important than you, and we desire hearts that love you alone. Help us to love you and worship you more than anything else. Thank you for your faithfulness to your people Israel. Keep us from idols that we might return to you. Give us ears to hear your messengers. Be near to those who have been forced out of their homelands and are living in exile today. We pray in the name of the Father, of the Son, and of the Holy Spirit. Amen.

Activity Options

Go outside and gather a handful of grass and leaves. Put them all in a big pile together. Talk about how God's people were all together, just like this. They were in the Promised Land, but they ignored the warnings from the prophets and instead continued in their disobedience of God. Next, blow on the pile of grass and leaves. Explain the object lesson: that just like the leaves and grass were scattered, God's people were also scattered and exiled after they persisted in their disobedience. They were separated from each other and forced out of the Promised Land.

Reach out to someone who has been forced out of their homeland by war, famine, or any other type of danger. If you don't already know of anyone, find a refugee outreach organization and ask about opportunities to donate supplies, make cards, or put together baskets to welcome families who are new to your area. You can also ask about opportunities to help, attend events, and make friends with someone from a foreign land. Ask them all about their home, and welcome them to yours.

Isaiah: Messiah Foretold

Today's Scripture Reading: If your child or children are old enough to read, they can take turns reading the Scripture of the day.

"Who has believed what he has heard from us? And to whom has the arm of the Lord been revealed? For he grew up before him like a young plant, and like a root out of dry ground; he had no form or majesty that we should look at him, and no beauty that we should desire him" (Isaiah 53:1–2).

Sing "O Come, O Come, Emmanuel"

Video your kids to get them used to singing the song in front of the camera. This will allow you to get a great clip to post on social media on Christmas Eve.

134

STORY

The Messiah Foretold (Isaiah)

One of the most powerful books of the Bible is the Old Testament book of Isaiah. Isaiah warned of the coming judgment to the Southern Kingdom because they would not stop their great idolatry. But more than any other Old Testament book, Isaiah speaks of the Messiah who would one day save Israel and bring peace and safety. Do you remember what a messiah is? **A messiah is an anointed or "chosen one" who will deliver or save a people.**

Wouldn't you say that God's special people need someone to deliver them from all their problems? It just doesn't seem like they have what it takes to follow God. Nobody understood everything Isaiah said, especially that the Messiah would be a light to all nations, not just the Jewish people. But amazingly, Isaiah said the Messiah would not come as a mighty warrior or political leader, but as a suffering servant. Isaiah 53:2–5 states,

> *"For he grew up before him like a young plant, and like a root out of dry ground; he had no form or majesty that we should look at him, and no beauty that we should desire him. He was despised and rejected by men, a man of sorrows and acquainted with grief; and as one from whom men hide their faces he was despised, and we esteemed him not."*

Isaiah says that unlike someone like King Saul, this messiah would not look like a mighty leader and that he would be rejected by men. Let's keep reading.

> *"Surely he has borne our griefs and carried our sorrows; yet we esteemed him stricken, smitten by God, and afflicted. But he was pierced for our transgressions; he was crushed for our iniquities; upon him was the chastisement that brought us peace, and with his wounds we are healed."*

Again, Isaiah says the Messiah will not be treated wonderfully. Instead, he will be mistreated, but that will be for the benefit of the people. This suffering will bring peace and healing. So, does God describe the Messiah as a mighty leader, or as someone we wouldn't expect? **As someone we wouldn't expect.**

So during exile, the darkest time in the history of God's people, when it seemed like hope was a faint whisper, God says a Messiah is coming. Isaiah says he will be born of a virgin, that God's Spirit would rest on him, and that he would be called Immanuel, which means "God with us."

Are we finally beginning to understand how special this time of the year is? Are we starting to see that God's special people are a driving force behind Advent? There are hints of God's love for Gentiles, but so far all the stories point to the need for a Jewish Messiah. God's people just can't get it right—over and over they turn from God, even though he has delivered them mightily and dwelt among them like with no other people. So far, is the Bible mainly teaching about the Jewish people or about Gentiles? **Jewish people.** Do you think God is also working on a plan that will help Gentiles? **I think so too.**

Memory Verse: If your child or children are old enough to read, they can take turns reading the memory verse of the day.

> *"The light shines in the darkness, and the darkness has not overcome it" (John 1:5).*

"shines" – make fists with your arms folded, then explode hands open as you raise your hands over your head
"not" - shake head no

Pray

God our King, we praise you because you are like no other. There is no person, no god, nobody and nothing that compares to you. Thank you for this Messiah who is like no other.

Thank you for the beautiful promises you give to your people when they are hopeless. Every one of us has turned to our own way. Thank you for the suffering servant who did not sin but brought forever deliverance by taking our sin and the punishment for our sin. Help us to know and understand your word and promises, and to love this Messiah more and more. May we see as you see. Bless us these next few days as we think about the promise of God with us—the coming of our Messiah. We pray in the name of the Father, of the Son, and of the Holy Spirit. Amen.

Activity

Play a flashlight game. Set up a completely dark room with a flashlight and Bible hidden in it. Have everyone try to find the flashlight and Bible in the dark. After some time searching, get the flashlight and turn it on. While still in the dark room, use the flashlight for someone to read Isaiah 9:2, 6–7. Talk about how the Messiah who was foretold in Isaiah was promised to be a great light for people walking in deep darkness. How does it feel to be in the darkness and then to have light finally shine? What was the deep darkness that the people were walking in? Why was the Messiah called a great light?

Day 23

Exiles Return

Today's Scripture Reading: If your child or children are old enough to read, they can take turns reading the Scripture of the day.

> *"For if you return to the LORD, your brothers and your children will find compassion with their captors and return to this land. For the LORD your God is gracious and merciful and will not turn away his face from you, if you return to him" (2 Chronicles 30:9).*

Sing "O Come, O Come, Emmanuel"

Video your family singing the entire song, and send the video to a relative or family you won't see this Christmas.

STORY

Exiles Return and Temple Rebuilt—God's Spirit Absent

The people of Israel were exiled, but God never forgot about them. The prophet Jeremiah told God's people after seventy years in captivity, he would return his people to their land. God always fulfills his promises. So after seventy years, Cyrus, the king of Persia, made a proclamation allowing God's people to return to their land and rebuild the Temple in Jerusalem. I am not sure if you got that last part, so I am going to say it again. Not only did God fulfill his promise of returning his people back to the land in the time he said, but he also put it into the foreign king's heart for them to rebuild their temple. After seventy years, what did Jeremiah say would happen to his people? **They would return to their land.**

It had been so long since God's people had been together as one people that they had forgotten God's Torah (instructions). But one thing they did know to do was to repair the altar and make a sacrifice to God, so that is exactly the first thing they did. It took two long years to lay the foundation for this second temple. Why do you think the people wanted to rebuild the temple? **They wanted God to live with them again.**

When the Jewish people were exiled out of Jerusalem, new people moved in. These people did not like that the Jews returned, so they tried to stir up trouble for God's people. And when a new king took over, they wrote a letter telling him the Jews were rebuilding the temple, in hopes he would stop the work. But nothing can stop God. When the new king found the old king's decree, instead of stopping the work, he gave the Jews the money needed to rebuild the Temple. He decreed that anything and everything needed would be totally funded from the royal treasury. It took twenty years to rebuild the Temple and when it was finally finished God's people celebrated its dedication. Hundreds of sacrifices were made, and in perfect timing they also celebrated the Lord's Passover. What did the people celebrate when they finally finished rebuilding the Temple? **The Lord's Passover.**

But even with the great joy that came from celebrating the finishing of the Temple, there was still something missing. First off, this new Temple was not as big as the first one. But what was really missing was God's presence filling it as before. Due to Israel's continued disobedience, when the Temple that Solomon built was destroyed, one thing that was lost forever was the Ark of the Covenant. The Ark was where God's presence rested, so without it the Temple was incomplete. As great as it was to return to the land God promised, and as great as it was to rebuild the Temple, nothing compared to having God's presence. What was missing that left the Temple incomplete? **The Ark of the Covenant.** Israel learned that God's presence was needed more than a building.

Memory Verse: If your child or children are old enough to read, they can take turns reading the memory verse of the day.

> *"The light shines in the darkness, and the darkness has not overcome it"*
> *(John 1:5).*

"shines" – make fists with your arms folded then explode hands open as you raise your
  hands over your head
"not" - shake head "no"

Pray
Faithful God, we praise you because you always keep your promises. Thank you that you faithfully brought your people out of exile and back into their home. Thank you that nothing can stop your plan. Just like your people needed you to fill the Temple and live with them, we say today that we need you to live with us. Forgive us when we forget how much we need you. We ask you to always be with us. We ask you to give us patience and trust when we need to wait for you. May you be known, loved, and worshipped. We pray in the name of the Father, of the Son, and of the Holy Spirit. Amen.

Activity

Read together interactively. Find or make something to represent many people. This could be dolls/action figures, game pieces, people created out of paper or cardboard, etc. You could even act it out using your own family members, if desired. Get into a good spot to read together and set up the many people. Set some of them up in a group all together in the middle to represent Israel—the Jewish people, God's chosen people. Then set up some people far away, spread outside the group, to represent foreigners, or Gentiles. Explain to your children that the middle group is the Jews and the spread-out people are Gentiles. Ask them to listen to the reading and figure out what God is saying about the Gentiles. Once you're set up, read Isaiah 56:1–8 out loud. Discuss the passage and the promises God makes in it. Reread it if helpful. Ask your kids to show you what God says will happen to the Gentiles who are faithful to him and move the people who represent the foreigners into the middle group alongside the Jews.

Day 24

Announcement to Mary

Today's Scripture Reading: If your child or children are old enough to read, they can take turns reading the Scripture of the day.

> *"'She will bear a son, and you shall call his name Jesus, for he will save his people from their sins.' All this took place to fulfill what the Lord had spoken by the prophet: 'Behold, the virgin shall conceive and bear a son, and they shall call his name Immanuel'" (Matthew 1:21–23).*

Sing "O Come, O Come, Emmanuel"
Post a clip of your family singing with the hashtag #GospelAdventBook

STORY

Announcement of Yeshua to Mary (Luke 1, Matthew 1)

Note to parents: If children ask what a virgin is, you can simply say that it takes a mommy and a daddy to have a baby, and a virgin is a girl who has never joined together with a daddy. Of course, this answer is intended to be just enough for you to continue with the story and is not intended to fully explain things.

OK, it is Christmas Eve. We are almost there. We are almost to Christmas!

We learned yesterday that Israel did return from exile and did rebuild the Temple, but God's presence was missing. And not only did they have to do without God's presence, but soon after the completion of the Temple, God stopped sending any prophets. For four hundred years, God was silent.

But when life seemed darkest, in his perfect timing God sent the angel Gabriel with a message. Gabriel did not go to a ruler, priest, or king. Gabriel went to the city of Nazareth, to a young virgin named Mary from the tribe of Judah. We all know her as Mary, but her actual Hebrew name was Miriam. But so we don't get too distracted, we will just continue calling her Mary. "Greetings, O favored one, the Lord is with you!" was how Gabriel greeted Miriam.

Naturally, Mary was startled, but Gabriel told her not to be afraid because she had found favor with God. "And behold, you will conceive in your womb and bear a son, and you shall call his name Yeshua. He will be great and will be called Son of the Most High. And the Lord God will give him the throne of his father David, and he will reign over the house of Jacob forever, and of his kingdom there will be no end." Does anyone know what Yeshua means? **Yeshua is Hebrew and it means salvation.** What emotions do you think Mary felt when an angel told her she was going to have a baby and to name him salvation?

Mary asked how she could have a child since she was an unmarried virgin. The angel told her that the power of the Most High would overshadow her and she would conceive a child. Mary responded in belief, saying, "Let it be to me according to your word," and rejoiced in song over what God was going to do through her. How did the angel tell Mary she would conceive a child without a daddy? **The power of the Most High would overshadow her.**

But Mary was engaged to a man named Joseph, so having a child that was not his was quite a problem. Most men in that time would have ended the engagement, but once again, God sent an angel, this time to Joseph, and told him to continue his marriage plans with Mary. Months later, just as God said, Mary gave birth to a son: Yeshua. What does Yeshua mean? **Salvation.**

With that, God's plan to come down from heaven and save his chosen people had begun. Yeshua, the deliverer that the nation of Israel had been waiting for, was coming. Over and over again, they had failed God. But over and over, God had shown himself faithful to his promises. And now, after being silent for so long, God sent a message that salvation was coming. But incredibly, this Jewish Messiah that God was sending was also the deliverer for the rest of the world—a deliverer we didn't even know we needed. Even before he had chosen a people, God had promised that someone born of a woman would crush the enemy. Remember that? This baby is not just a baby, he is salvation. Can anyone name a story when God gave a shadow of his love for the Gentiles? **Ruth, Jericho, and Jonah.**

Memory Verse: If your child or children are old enough to read, they can take turns reading the memory verse of the day.

"In the beginning was the Word, and the Word was with God, and the Word was God. He was in the beginning with God. All things were

made through him, and without him was not any thing made that
was made. In him was life, and the life was the light of men.
The light shines in the darkness, and the darkness has
not overcome it" (John 1:1–5).

"beginning" - (pretend to) point to your wristwatch

"Word" - make your hands into a book

"with" – make and OK sign with both hands and connect them like chain links

"God" – make your hands into a book and lift them to the sky

"beginning" – (pretend to) point to your wristwatch

"God" – point upward

"all" – stretch your arms out wide

"made" – pretend to be a carpenter using a hammer to make something

"without" – make an "x" with your arms

"not any thing" – shake your head no

"life" – make a heart shape with your hands

"light" – make the sun by placing your hands above your head in a circle

"shines" – make fists with your arms folded, then explode your hands open as you raise your hands over your head

"not" – shake your head "no"

Pray

God with us, we praise you because you are holy. We thank you that in mercy, you made a way to live with us. Thank you for Mary's obedience and faith. Help us have her faith when we have to wait for you. We need you. We need Yeshua. We are in need of your salvation. Thank you for coming to your people. Please come again soon. We pray in the name of the Father, of the Son, and of the Holy Spirit. Amen.

Activity

Waiting. Together, make a quick sketch or list and review all of the people we've talked about this month who had to wait—often a long time—for God: Noah, Abraham, Joseph, the Israelites (again and again), Joshua, Jonah, Mary, and more. Next, light incense and talk about how incense symbolizes prayers rising to God. God often asks his people to wait a long time for his promises to be fulfilled, but he is always faithful to fulfill them in his perfect timing! As we eagerly wait for many things in our own lives—like waiting for a seed to sprout, cookies to bake, long lines, Christmas morning to come, or most importantly, for Jesus to return—remember how many long centuries the Jews waited for that very first Christmas, the day when the long-promised Messiah finally came. Through our prayers and incense, we join with all the saints who have gone before us in waiting on God. Sit in silence and meditate on this.

Birth of Yeshua

Today's Scripture Reading: If your child or children are old enough to read, they can take turns reading the Scripture of the day.

"For unto you is born this day in the city of David a Savior, who is Christ the Lord. And this will be a sign for you: you will find a baby wrapped in swaddling cloths and lying in a manger" (Luke 2:11–12).

Sing "Joy to the World" and dance! You can stream the song on a device or online if you don't know the words. If desired, let your children ring Christmas bells or play other celebratory instruments.

Post a clip of your family singing the song with the hashtag #GospelAdventBook

STORY

The Birth of Yeshua (Jesus) – Christmas Day

We're here—it is finally Christmas morning! This is what we have been moving toward for the last few weeks.

After Joseph and Mary were married, Caesar Augustus, the ruler of Rome, decreed that everyone had to return to their hometown to be counted. This meant that Joseph and Mary would have to leave Nazareth and travel to Bethlehem. But by the time they made it to Bethlehem, Mary was ready to give birth. However, there was no place for them to stay. So, with no place to stay, Mary gave birth to Yeshua, wrapped him in swaddling clothes, and laid him in a manger. Who remembers what the name Yeshua means? **Salvation.** All of history had led to this moment, and you would think God would gather important people from around the world to see his son. But just like the rest of the world did not know their savior was coming, Israel didn't expect their Messiah to come so quietly and in such a low manner.

God did gather some people, but not the people we would think. Out in the fields, in the dark of night, some shepherds were watching their flock. With the glory of the Lord shining all around, an angel appeared to them. Naturally, they were filled with fear, but the angel said, "Fear not, for behold, I bring you good news of great joy that will be for all people. For unto you is born this day, in the city of David a Savior, who is Messiah (Christ) the Lord."

And when the angel finished speaking, a multitude of angels filled the sky praising God. So, when the angels left, the shepherds went and found the baby Yeshua right where they were told. They shared with Joseph and Mary all the angels had told them. As you can imagine a mother would do, Mary treasured every word in her heart. After seeing God's salvation wrapped in flesh, the shepherds returned to their flock, praising God for all they had seen and heard. And now, Israel, God's chosen people who had constantly turned from him, had no idea that God had finally sent their Messiah. Did Israel know God had finally sent their Messiah? **No.**

The birth of Yeshua certainly gives us insight into how different God's plan is than how we would do things. Today, we celebrate the birth of Yeshua, the Jewish Messiah that God mercifully sent to save us from our sins. Just as his chosen people sin by turning from him, our sin keeps us from knowing his great love. And just as the nation of Israel went to sleep that night not knowing that God's salvation had come, many will go to sleep tonight not knowing that the same salvation God sent for Israel also came for them. God's mercy came down from Heaven to rescue us before we even knew we needed him. We can love because he loved us first.

Who was waiting for a savior, Jews or Gentiles? **Jews.** Did the Gentiles know they needed a savior? **No.** Right, the Gentiles did not even know they needed a savior. And since we are Gentiles, it makes sense that we should be the most excited about Yeshua's coming. This Jewish Messiah came from heaven, and in the quiet of the night, God sent his son and brought light into darkness.

Memory Verse: If your child or children are old enough to read, they can take turns reading the memory verse of the day.

> *"In the beginning was the Word, and the Word was with God, and the Word was God. He was in the beginning with God. All things were made through him, and without him was not any thing made that was made. In him was life, and the life was the light of men. The light shines in the darkness, and the darkness has not overcome it" (John 1:1–5).*

"beginning" - (pretend to) point to your wristwatch
"Word" – make your hands into a book

"with" – make an OK sign with both hands and connect them like chain links

"God" – make your hands into a book and lift them to the sky

"beginning" – (pretend to) point to your wristwatch

"God" – point upward

"all" – stretch your arms out wide

"made" – pretend to be a carpenter using a hammer to make something

"without" – make an "x" with your arms

"not any thing" – shake your head "no"

"life" – make a heart shape with your hands

"light" – make the sun by placing your hands above your head in a circle

"shines" – make fists with your arms folded, then explode hands open as you raise your hands over your head

"not" - shake head "no"

Pray

God of Salvation, we praise you because you are both fully God and fully human. Thank you for sending your son to the earth as the only perfect Messiah who can save us from our sin. We confess that there are many times when we don't notice you in our lives because the way you come to us doesn't look like what we would expect. Help us have open hearts and open eyes so that we might see you with us, just like the shepherds, Mary, and Joseph did. Today we remember your coming, and we ask you to come again soon. We pray in the name of the Father, of the Son, and of the Holy Spirit. Amen.

Activity

Sing the "Happy Birthday" song to Jesus. If desired, bake a cake and/or other celebratory foods to celebrate the Messiah on this feast day!

Day 25 – Evening

Blessing to Gentiles

Today's Scripture Reading: If your child or children are old enough to read, they can take turns reading the Scripture of the day.

"Christ redeemed us from the curse of the law by becoming a curse for us—
for it is written, 'Cursed is everyone who is hanged on a tree'—so
that in Christ Jesus the blessing of Abraham might come to the Gentiles, so that
we might receive the promised Spirit through faith" (Galatian 3:13–14).

Sing "Joy to the World" and dance! If desired, let your children ring Christmas bells or play other celebratory instruments.

158

STORY

Jesus's Life, Death, Resurrection, and the Spirit is Given to the Gentiles (Christmas Evening)

OK, this is going to be a lot of information, so who thinks they can listen well and get all of the questions right without help?

Eventually, Yeshua grew up and came to the Jewish people. He chose twelve disciples and taught them about the Kingdom of God. But even though he performed many miracles and lived a life full of love, his own people did not receive him as Messiah. He fulfilled all the prophecies given by the prophets about the Messiah, but the nation of Israel still rejected him. Did the Jewish people accept Yeshua as Messiah? **No.** Eventually, the Jewish leaders handed Yeshua over to the Roman ruler, asking him to crucify Yeshua. Yeshua was tortured, mocked, and died on a cross. But after being buried he rose from the dead three days later in power. After being killed and buried, did Yeshua remain dead? **No.**

After Jesus rose from the dead, he told the disciples to go to Jerusalem and wait for the promise of the Holy Spirit. In times before, the Spirit of God (the Holy Spirit) would dwell in the Temple above the Ark of the Covenant. But now God's Spirit would actually dwell inside his people. The disciples went to Jerusalem, gathered in an upper room, and it was there that they were all filled with the Holy Spirit. Where would the Holy Spirit dwell? **In God's people.**

But remember God's promise to Abraham? God told him that he would be a blessing to all nations. For all the years up until now, Israel was the only one who had special access to God, but now everything was changing. No longer would the world (Gentiles) be on the outside with no hope.

God gave a vision to the disciple named Peter and a Gentile named Cornelius who feared God, and then brought them together. Anyone know what a vision is? A vision is like seeing a dream, only you're awake instead of asleep. It was during the meeting of Peter and Cornelius that God gave his Spirit to those who were without hope. As Peter was talking with Cornelius, the Holy Spirit fell on the Gentiles just like on the Jews. For so many years Gentiles were far from God, but now, because of Yeshua's sacrifice, the Spirit of God could make them clean and empower them just like the Jews. Can Gentiles have God's Spirit dwell in them now? **Yes.**

The birth of Yeshua is spectacular because with his coming, God fulfilled his promise to provide a Messiah to his people. But it is even more spectacular for the world because God sent Yeshua into the world to bless all the nations. God gave us what we did not know we needed—a savior and the gift of his Spirit. Now that is Good News!

Memory Verse: If your child or children are old enough to read, they can take turns reading the memory verse of the day.

Go back over any or all verses memorized.

Pray

Father, we praise you because you are faithful and always keep your promises. Thank you for sending Yeshua so that Gentiles could also receive salvation from sin and be connected to your special people. Thank you for the gift of the Holy Spirit. We ask now that you would fill us and live with us. Protect us from rejecting you like the Jewish leaders did. May we keep the true meaning of Christmas in our hearts and minds every day of the year. We ask for more people all over the world to know your love, truth, and forgiveness that they might be saved. We thank you for coming to your people, and we pray for you to come again to us soon. We pray in the name of the Father, of the Son, and of the Holy Spirit. Amen.

Activity

Read together interactively. Use a piece of paper to symbolize the dividing wall of hostility between the Jews and Gentiles. Put little people made out of one color of Play-Doh on one side of the wall to be the Jews. Put little people made out of another color of Play-Doh on the other side of the wall to represent the Gentiles. Read Ephesians 3:11–22, and reread if desired. After reading, demonstrate what Yeshua did by destroying the dividing wall (paper) and combining the Jews and Gentiles into one. Talk about how this is what Christmas makes possible! Yeshua's birth, life, death, and resurrection means that now, unlike in the past, ALL people can be included in God's kingdom of peace and enter into his family through faith in Yeshua.

Story of Advent

Let's say you didn't have time to finish all the readings in this book. That's OK—this time of year is always busy. But I'd like for you to have all of the readings in story form to use in a way that benefits your family. That "story" is what follows.

This story is not intended to be used if you have been able to read through most of this book. This story is a stand-alone version intended to be used in place of all the stories in this book. For instance, if you started this book and were unable to continue, but wanted to do something other than read the Christmas story on Christmas day, this story would be a great option. In essence, this is a summary of the Bible through the birth of the Messiah.

* * *

The story of the Bible is the story of the world. The story of the Bible is not just a collection of stories that are not connected. The Bible gives us an understanding of everything we need to know about God, how he made things work, and how much he loves all his creation. Christmas is a special time for us, but if we understand the real story that leads up to the birth of Jesus (Yeshua), then we can really appreciate how grateful we should be each year. So, here is the story of the Bible up to what we are celebrating today.

In the beginning God created the heaven and earth in six days, and he rested on the seventh day. That means God created the sun, the moon, birds, land animals, and fish in the sea, all in six days. He also created Adam and Eve on the sixth day and placed them in a garden. Our first parents were made in God's image and just like all God's creation was good, they were created good. God created the heaven and earth in how many days? **Six.**

God gave Adam and Eve the authority to govern the whole earth and told them to be fruitful and multiply. They were allowed to eat anything of the garden except the Tree of the Knowledge of Good and Evil. But one day, Satan the deceiver came and tempted them to eat of the tree. When they gave in to temptation, sin and death came into the world. What came into the world when they gave in to temptation? **Sin and death.**

God responded to their sin by cursing the ground and casting them from the garden, but he also said that one day a man would come to crush the enemy. God's love story of rescuing people from their failures is a story we read about again and again.

Sin entering the world broke the goodness of God's world, and soon things got so bad that he decided to destroy everything and everyone with a great flood. But God rescued one man and his family from the flood. God had a man named Noah build a great boat called an ark and bring all kinds of animals onto the ark before the flood began. Because Noah obeyed the instructions God gave, Noah, his family, and two of each kind of animal escaped death from the flood.

Years later, God called a man to leave his family and go to a land God told him about. He obeyed, and God changed his name to Abraham. God promised Abraham a land, that he would be a father to many nations, and that all the families of the earth would be blessed through him. Let me repeat that promise. God promised Abraham a land, that he would be a father to many nations, and that all the families of the earth would be blessed through him.

Abraham believed God, and even though he was too old to have a child, God gave him a son named Isaac. Isaac had a son named Jacob. OK, before we get too confused with names, let's stop and say something together. Say "the God of Abraham, Isaac, and Jacob." Say it with me again, "the God of Abraham, Isaac and Jacob." Who is he the God of? **Abraham, Isaac, and Jacob.**

OK, great. Now that we know Abraham, Isaac, and Jacob, let's move forward. So, Jacob had twelve sons, but he loved his son named Joseph more than the other sons. In anger, the brothers sold Joseph into slavery, and he ended up in Egypt. But God protected Joseph, and he eventually rose to second in command of all of Egypt.

God used Joseph to save the people of Egypt and his own family from a famine. A famine is when the land doesn't produce enough crops to feed the people in that area. Joseph's family moved to the land of Egypt, but hundreds of years later, out of fear, the Egyptians enslaved their descendants because they greatly multiplied.

But because he always keeps his promises, The God of Abraham, Isaac, and Jacob heard their cries to deliver them from slavery and sent a man named Moses to lead them out. In great power, God delivered the Hebrews from the Egyptians. God made the Hebrews into a nation we call Israel, and before giving Israel the land he promised, God gave them the Torah. The Torah was all the instructions for how they should live. God told them that if they obeyed the Torah and followed him alone, they would be blessed, but if they turned from him and followed pretend gods, he would remove them from the land. What does God say would happen if they turned from him? **He would remove them from the land.** We call this group of people Jewish and the rest of the world Gentiles. The Jewish people are God's special people, and for the most part Gentiles are not the focus of the stories in the Old Testament. But since God is so good, he always had a plan to show his goodness. But back to the story.

The people of Israel agreed to keep all the commands, and a man named Joshua led them into the land. After Joshua died, God raised up judges, which are temporary leaders, to lead Israel. But eventually the people rebelled against God and asked for a king like the other nations had.

God gave them King Saul, but he rebelled against God, so God chose a man named David to be king. David was not perfect, but he was Israel's mightiest king. Eventually, David's son Solomon became king. Solomon built a Temple where God's presence rested. The temple was spectacular, but because Solomon led the people to worship pretend gods, God divided Israel into two kingdoms. The people kept turning to pretend gods instead of being faithful to the one true God. Over and over God sent prophets who called the people back to serving God alone. But over and over the people rebelled against God. Eventually God sent foreign armies to conquer Israel. The Temple where God's presence once dwelled was destroyed, and the Israelites were exiled from the land of promise just like God said. What did God do when Israel kept turning to pretend gods? **He exiled them from their land.**

But God remembered his promise to Abraham, Isaac, and Jacob and brought some of the people back to the land. They rebuilt the Temple, but God's presence did not dwell there like before, and for four hundred years God was silent. But the silence was broken when God sent the angel Gabriel to a woman named Mary. The angel told Mary that she would have a son and that she should name him Yeshua because he would save his people. *Yeshua* means salvation. With God being silent for so long, the Israelites were waiting for a mighty deliverer. They were waiting for an anointed one or messiah sent by God to restore the Kingdom and lead the people.

Over and over, year after year, the people turned from God. But over and over, God remained faithful to his promises. But while the people were waiting for a political or military deliverer, in just the right time, God sent the angel Gabriel with a message.

But Gabriel did not go to a ruler, priest or king. Gabriel went to a young virgin named Mary. Who did God send the angel Gabriel to? **Mary.**

Naturally, Mary was startled but Gabriel told her not to be afraid, because she had found favor with God. "And behold, you will conceive in your womb and bear a son, and you shall call his name Yeshua. He will be great and will be called Son of the Most High. And the Lord God will give him the throne of his father David, and he will reign over the house of Jacob forever, and of his kingdom there will be no end." Does anyone know what *Yeshua* means? ***Yeshua* is Hebrew and means salvation.**

Mary asked how this could be since she was an unmarried virgin. The angel told her that the power of the Most High would overshadow her and she would conceive a child. Mary responded in belief, saying, "Let it be to me according to your word." How did the angel tell Mary she would conceive a child without a daddy? **The power of the Most High would overshadow her.**

But Mary was engaged to a man named Joseph, so having a child that was not his was quite a problem. Most men in that time would have ended the engagement, but once again, God sent an angel, this time to Joseph, and told him to keep his marriage plans with Mary. Months later, just as God had said, Mary gave birth to a son: Yeshua. What does *Yeshua* mean? **Salvation.**

After Joseph and Mary were married, the ruler of Rome decreed that everyone must return to their hometown to be counted. This meant that Mary and Joseph would have to leave Nazareth and travel to Bethlehem. But by the time they made it to Bethlehem, Mary was ready to give birth. However, there was no place for them to stay. So, with no place to stay, Mary gave birth to Yeshua, wrapped him in swaddling clothes, and laid him in a manger. Who remembers what the name *Yeshua* means? **Salvation.** All of history had led to this moment, and Israel didn't expect their Messiah to come so quietly and in such a low manner, but that is what happened. God's people could not follow God completely, so in mercy he sent his son to deliver them.

The birth of Yeshua certainly gives us insight into how different God's plan is than how we would do things. Today we celebrate the birth of Yeshua, the Jewish Messiah whom God mercifully sent to save us from our sins. Just as his chosen people sin by turning from him, our sin keeps us from knowing his great love. Just as the nation of Israel went to sleep that night not knowing that God's salvation had come, many will go to sleep tonight not knowing that the same salvation God sent for Israel also came for them. God's mercy came down from Heaven to rescue us before we even knew we needed him. We can love because he loved us first.

Who was waiting for a savior, Jews or Gentiles? **Jews.** Did the Jews realize God had sent a savior? **No.** Did the Gentiles know they needed a savior? **No.** Right, the Gentiles did not even know they needed a savior. And since we are Gentiles, it makes sense that we should be the most excited about Yeshua's coming. This Jewish Messiah came from heaven, and in the quiet of the night, God sent his son and brought light into darkness. Yeshua came to not only save his people, but God sent his son so that through him, salvation would also come to the Gentiles. Yeshua is the man whom God told Adam and Eve would crush the enemy. Tonight, we celebrate God sending his son to fix all that was broken.

Additional Resources

Advent Resources

Adult

God Is in the Manger, Dietrich Bonhoeffer

The Dawning of Indestructible Joy: Daily Readings for Advent, John Piper

Come Let Us Adore Him, Paul David Tripp

Family

The Advent Book, Jack Stockman

The Advent Jesse Tree: Devotions for Children and Adults to Prepare for the Coming of the Christ Child at Christmas, Dean Lambert Smith

The Advent Storybook, Laura Richie

Unwrapping the Greatest Gift: A Family Celebration of Christmas, Ann Voskamp

Check our website for downloads: www.wydenpublishing.com.

Other Books by Chris Chavez

The Family Discipleship Bible

A Forever Family for Antonio: A Gospel Adoption Journey

Vanity, Vanity, American Christianity: Chasing the Wind

Acknowledgments

Jen Windle – Your artwork truly captured the vision, and your sole desire to glorify God with your paintings fueled each piece. For years to come these paintings will point others to Jesus, and I am grateful to God for bringing you to this project.

Sarah Damoff – Your help, hints, and singular focus is what helped bring this book to life. I knew early on that you are whom I wanted to work with, and you absolutely delivered. Thank you so much for helping to create a depth of spirituality that will be felt by families around the world. My hope is that in the future, you publish not only your personal story but the other ideas swimming around in your head. You are a true blessing to the downtrodden and to the Kingdom.

Sarah Damoff was born and raised in the Dallas-Fort Worth metroplex of Texas. She grew up with a single, blind mother who passed away suddenly when Sarah was a teen. She has a BS in Development and Family Studies from the University of North Texas. She has been a children's minister, a teacher in North India, and an Educational Counselor. She is currently a wife, mother of three, freelance writer, and Dallas Court-Appointed Special Advocate.

Jen Windle lives in Denton, Texas, with her husband of 13 years and two precious sons. Her prayer is that her art would glorify the Lord and that He would use it to call His children to Himself. She is thankful to have been a part of this book and grateful to her family and friends who have prayed for her and supported her throughout the process.

secor.cc
Buy Ink. End Human Trafficking.

Secor.cc was created to allow you to make a real difference to real people with a purchase you are already making.

We have devoted our company, our experience and expertise, and our products completely to the cause of fighting human trafficking and restoring its victims.

100% of the profit on all purchases of printer cartridges at www.secor.cc is given to non-profits who are fighting human trafficking.

9 781632 962676